The Neck & Back Pain Solution

Everything You Need to Know About Non-Surgical Spinal Decompression Therapy

Dr. Jonathan Donath, DC, MS

The Neck & Back Pain Solution:
Everything You Need to Know
About Non-Surgical Spinal Decompression Therapy
ISBN: 978-0-9861281-5-8
Author: Dr. Jonathan Donath, DC, MS

3rd Printing December 2020
Printed in the United States of America

Dedication

To my parents, Dr. Max and Paulette Donath

I thank G-d every day that I won the lottery and got the two of you as my parents. You're the best role models I could have ever hoped for. Growing up the son of a renowned professor of mechanical engineering who got his PhD from MIT, and an occupational therapist who did her training at Columbia and Johns Hopkins Universities, one would think I would have had a lot of pressure to succeed. From the time I was a kid, all the way through adulthood, you never forced me into any one direction. You were strict when you needed to be but always fair and compassionate. You gave me unconditional love and support and were behind me 100% in every decision I ever made. You taught me the meaning of hard work and dedication to your craft. If you're going to do something - strive to be the best at it. It's such a comforting feeling knowing that no matter what, you are in my corner. If Meira and I can be half the parents that you were to me, my kids will be in excellent shape. I love you both very much.

To my wife, Meira

You are an incredible wife and an even better mother.

I don't know what I did right to deserve you but I am so thankful that I have you as my partner. No matter how high the risk, you have always supported me in everything I do and every decision I have made. You have taken care of literally everything at home so I could focus on helping patients get out of pain or work on my book. You even support my golf habit. Who does that?!? In addition, you always try to get me to stop and take a minute to be proud of my accomplishments. I would not have been able to accomplish half of them without you. I am proud of our joint accomplishments and even prouder to be your young trophy-husband. I don't say it often enough, but I truly appreciate everything you do for me and our kids. I have now known you for more than half of my life. My love for you grows stronger and stronger with every passing year.

To my son, Eitan, and my daughter, Talia

I am so proud to be your father. You are growing up to be incredible individuals. I cannot wait to see what you both become, yet I am in absolutely no rush to get there. Treat others at least as well as you'd like to be treated yourselves. Follow your dreams whatever they may be. Remember that if you truly love what you do, you'll never have to work a day in your life. You both are my everything.

Acknowledgments

When I set out to write this book around 4 years ago I had no idea what I was getting myself into. So much time and detail go into every word and phrase and without the following people I don't think it would have ever been completed.

Special thanks to my right hand woman for the past 4 years, April Matos. April started out as my spinal decompression patient and later became my assistant. She's edited countless copies of the manuscript and always gave me great advice and input.

Special thanks also goes to Jana Warren, my editor the last year. I was really stuck until I met you. You were a pleasure to work with and a consummate professional in every way. I'm very thankful to have worked with you.

Thank you to Paul Streitz. Paul is an accomplished author and after helping him, he insisted that I must write a book on spinal decompression therapy. His persistent insistence is what got me to begin this project.

I have tremendous gratitude to the following doctors that have had a huge influence on shaping me as a doctor and on the way I practice:

Dr. Marc Arnel, Dr. Matt Berry, Dr. Scott Duke, Dr. Anthony Lisi, Dr. Joseph Manella, Dr. Keith Overland, Dr. Stephen Perle, and Dr. David Podell.

Dr. Perle and Dr. Lisi were so helpful when I needed to find certain research papers. In particular, I'd like to thank Dr. Overland, an unbelievable chiropractor and an even better man, who spent a lot of time reading the manuscript and giving me excellent advice.

I'd like to thank Dr. Cory Ferguson and the American Spinal Decompression Association for providing me with countless studies on discs and spinal decompression. (www.americanspinal.com.)

I am especially grateful to Ira Bedzow PhD. Dr. Bedzow is the director of the Biomedical Ethics and Humanities department at New York Medical College. He is a renowned author and linguist expert to name a few of his outstanding qualities. Not only did he read my unpublished manuscript but his advice was essential to the finished product.

A special shout out to Roger Del Russo from Roger Del Russo Photography for all the photographs in the book. And to Tim Thayer from Eyebuzz Design for his work on the pump mechanism graphic.

And a special thank you to Beth Gibney-Boulden for "modeling" all the exercises in the book. If you ever want to take a yoga class with a true master, look up Beth. She is beloved by all.

I would be remiss if I didn't mention Dr. Kavita Rambarat, Dr. Arthur Raisfeld, soon-to-be Dr. Ashley Narain, and Shlomo Ressler for their contributions and proof reading with regards to this book.

Last but not least, I would like to acknowledge and thank the thousands of patients who have walked through my office doors and trusted me to care for them.

About The Author

– Written by Healthcare News –Top Doctors of Westchester –appearing in the March 2014 Issue of Westchester County Healthcare News.

Dr. Jonathan Donath is regarded as one of the most respected chiropractors in the tri-state area. His reach spans much further than this region, however.

Dr. Donath prides himself on practicing evidenced-based medicine with a variety of proven techniques. Each treatment program is individually designed and prescribed for patients. Dr. Donath who has been in private practice for more than seven years, provides every patient with the best quality, compassionate and comprehensive care possible.

His diversified healthcare plans are individually tailored to each specific need. He always strives to make patients feel and function as well as possible, while trying to provide relief from their symptoms quickly.   Dr. Donath aims not to just treat symptoms, but to look for the underlying cause of the problem and correct it.

Dr. Donath's diverse group of patients ranges from children, to professional athletes, to senior citizens. He treats every one of them with gentle, confident, and caring hands.

He is renowned as one of the top experts in the field of Non-surgical Spinal Decompression Therapy. This cutting-edge FDA-cleared treatment is even effective for the most severe herniated discs, sciatica, degenerative disc disease and failed back surgery cases. Dr. Donath has a high success rate helping patients who were told surgery was their only option.

Dr. Donath is certified and specializes in Active Release

Technique (ART). ART is one of the most effective treatments available for treating soft tissue injuries. This hands-on, non-invasive method is designed to break up adhesions and scar tissue that typically result from repetitive stress, overuse, and trauma. Dr. Donath is also experienced and certified in Graston Technique, a patented form of instrument-assisted soft tissue mobilization that enables clinicians to effectively break down scar tissue and fascial restrictions. The technique utilizes specially designed stainless steel instruments to specifically detect and effectively treat areas exhibiting soft tissue fibrosis or chronic inflammation. Some conditions that are commonly improved by ART and Graston Technique include headaches/migraines, back and neck pain, tennis elbow, carpal tunnel syndrome, plantar fasciitis, TMJ pain as well as most types of tendonitis.

Dr. Donath also utilizes Cold Laser therapy, a treatment that employs specific wavelengths of light able to penetrate deep within tissue in order to help accelerate the healing process. Cold Laser therapy can stimulate all cell types including muscle, ligament, cartilage and nerves.

Dr. Donath is at the forefront of the Neil-Asher Technique, a revolutionary, safe, drug free, and proven treatment for frozen shoulders. It uses a unique process to break up the fibrotic tissue in patients' shoulders. Conventional approaches to treating Frozen Shoulders often involve painful injections, months of physical therapy and/or surgery.

In addition, Dr. Donath is highly-skilled in the Diversified Technique of manual joint manipulation. This efficient and effective technique is used to restore proper motion to an injured to "stuck" joint. It is a highly useful approach to restore proper joint function.

Whether it's attending the latest pain relieving technique seminars or reviewing the current literature, Dr. Donath strives to learn more about innovations in the field – in order to be the most qualified doctor for his patients. Medical doctors continue sending patients to Dr. Donath because he consistently gets their patients out of pain even when other therapies failed. Dr. Donath's results are fast. He is experienced, trustworthy, and does not prolong treatment with unnecessary procedures.

He is a frequent lecturer at Jacobi Medical Center in New York City. Dr. Donath graduated Summa Cum Laude from the University of Bridgeport College of Chiropractic and was the valedictorian of his class. He also has a Master's degree in Human Nutrition.

Table of Contents

1

Introduction

I decided to write this book to save you time, money, and most importantly, pain. I was inspired to do this because I felt there was a major problem, or more specifically, something missing within the traditional medical model for back and neck pain. People end up searching for alternative treatments for back and neck pain often after conventional medical treatment has not worked or only temporarily eases the pain.

There is a solution; I wish more people were aware that something can be done about back and neck pain and it doesn't have to (nor most times should it) include injections or surgery.

The types of pain I am speaking of include:

- back pain
- hip pain
- pain in the buttocks
- pain that shoots down the leg (also known as sciatica)
- foot pain
- neck pain
- shoulder pain
- arm pain
- and numbness and tingling in the arms or feet.

This pain can be dull and achy or it can be sharp and shooting. It can even burn so badly that it feels like someone is sticking a hot poker directly into your body. The pain can range from mild to severe, to absolutely crippling, where the patient cannot stand, walk or lie down without excruciating pain. Most of the more severe pains can be attributed to problems of the spine, and more specifically to bulging, herniated and degenerated discs.

The standard medical model has a very set protocol for treating these conditions but does not tackle the central problem - which is pressure on the nerves leading out of the spine, or pressure on the spinal cord itself. Very often the problem simply compounds, ultimately ending in surgery, which should only be considered as an absolute last resort.

Typically, when it comes to herniated discs, bulging discs, sciatica, degenerative disc disease, and spinal stenosis, the medical model proceeds as follows:

1. *Pain medication*
A patient first visits their primary care physician (PCP) with pain and the doctor prescribes a muscle relaxant, an anti-inflammatory, or both. If the problem is a simple muscle strain or spasm, then that may do the trick. In the majority of cases, however, when a disc is involved (and very often the issue does stem from a disc problem) medicine will not help, or, at best, it may merely take the edge off.

2. *Physical Therapy*
If the condition is not resolved, the patient often comes back to their doctor still in pain. Next, they are usually sent for physical therapy (PT). In some cases, PT will help. In a lot of disc cases, PT will not help, and will occasionally exacerbate the problem.

3. *Injections for pain management*
If the condition is still not resolved, the doctor will usually send them to a pain management doctor or physiatrist (a physical medicine doctor) who typically administers cortisone injections, epidurals, or nerve blocks, all of which are temporary "Band-Aids" that may alleviate the current pain, but not address the core problem. As a side note: patients are only allowed to receive a few cortisone shots

due to the long term destruction they can cause to the tissue involved as well as other potentially dangerous side-effects. In many cases the shots, which can be very painful, do absolutely nothing; in some cases, they can produce a tremendous amount of relief in the patient. Even when they do give relief, the relief will usually last only a few days or weeks. If the patient is particularly lucky, it may last a few months. The shots are not designed to fix the problem; they are solely for pain relief.

4. Surgery

The next step, after the above cycle of treatment options fail, is surgery. That is it. Unfortunately, surgery is not necessarily the solution. In fact, surgery to repair back issues has failed so often that the term "failed back surgery" is actually now a syndrome.

Medicine-Physical Therapy-Injections-Surgery. If surgery was a good option that worked well it would not be an issue; however, many people who have back or neck surgery end up needing to have multiple surgeries. Either surgery is required to clean up scar tissue from previous surgeries, or additional surgery is needed because the problem simply returns. The reason the problem returns is discussed throughout this book.

In writing this book I am trying to bring attention to non-surgical spinal decompression therapy, which helps a staggeringly high percentage of patients who otherwise have, or would have, failed to improve using all other forms of conventional treatment. Spinal decompression therapy is often able to get patients completely better and back to one hundred percent and it involves no surgery or medication.

Spinal decompression therapy offers a positive and

permanent solution to pain stemming from pressure put on the nerves by bulges or herniations. It does this by gently and painlessly sucking the bulges or herniations back into the disc. The disc can then return it to its natural position and resume its proper function. We will discuss this in great detail in a later chapter.

I have treated thousands of patients and enabled them to obtain long term relief from crippling pain in their back, legs, neck, and arms through spinal decompression therapy.

Before anyone with severe back or neck pain considers surgery, with all its associated risks and problems, they should have an examination with a doctor who specializes in spinal decompression therapy to find out if they are a candidate for this treatment.

2

Anatomy Lesson

Let me take a moment to explain how the spine works to provide you with support and flexibility, and what can go wrong with it and ultimately cause pain.

The anatomy of the low back and neck are very similar, except that the neck has smaller structures. Here, we'll discuss the lower back.

Important structures that are involved in lower back pain include the vertebrae, intervertebral discs (discs between the vertebrae), facet joints, ligaments around the spine and discs, spinal cord and nerves, and muscles of the low back.

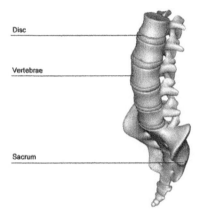

Disc

Vertebrae

Sacrum

The low back or lumbar spine is made up of five bones or vertebrae with discs between each vertebra. The vertebrae provides support while also protecting the spinal cord. The lumbar vertebrae stack immediately atop the sacrum bone that is situated in between the buttocks. On each side, the sacrum meets the iliac bone of the pelvis to form the sacroiliac joints (the largest joints in the body).

Facet joints, in conjunction with the discs, are what allow

the vertebrae to have flexibility. They allow the spine to bend forward, backward, and rotate.

Ligaments are strong, fibrous soft tissues that firmly attach bones to bones. Ligaments attach each of the vertebrae to each other and surround each of the discs.

The nerves that provide sensation and stimulate the muscles of the low back, as well as the thighs, legs, feet, and toes, exit the lumbar spinal column through "foramens", which are small bony portals.

Many muscle groups that are responsible for flexing, extending, and rotating the waist, as well as moving the lower extremities, attach to the lumbar spine.

The Disc

The disc is a pad that serves as a cushion between the individual vertebral bodies. They help to minimize the impact of stress forces on the spinal column. The disc is similar to a jelly donut. It has a central softer, jelly-like component called the *nucleus pulposus* which is made of water and nutrients. The disc is surrounded by harder outer rings of cartilage called the *annulus fibrosus*. The central portion of the disc is capable of bulging or herniating (rupturing) through the outer rings, causing major problems.

The discs have three main functions:

1. To act as a shock absorbers between adjoining vertebrae.
2. To act as joints that allow for mobility in the spine.
3. To act as ligaments that hold the vertebrae together.

When you break a bone in your arm your doctor puts you in a cast, and six weeks later your arm is healed. This is because bones have an excellent blood supply. Blood continuously brings nutrients to the bone, which promotes healing, and the healing proceeds quickly. What about when a football player, baseball player, or basketball player tears the ACL (anterior cruciate ligament) in one of their knees? Well, they typically miss an entire season. Why? Because the ACL is made of cartilage, and cartilage is avascular, which means there is no blood supply - there is no major vasculature leading in or out. The correlation between a torn ACL and a ruptured or herniated disc is that the disc is also made up of cartilage. **The only way discs get nutrients and nutrition is through something called the *pump mechanism* of disc nutrition**.

The pump mechanism is extremely important. When we walk, move, or exercise, there is a movement - a subtle up-and-down pumping motion - that causes water and nutrients to flow into the discs of the spine, and water and waste to flow back out. This pump mechanism is essential for keeping the discs healthy. When the pump mechanism gets altered, whether it is through a trauma like a car accident or a fall, repetitive motion, or just plain genetics, that is when back problems arise. Between the ages of 20 and 40 is when most people have their first back issue. Whatever that first "uh oh" moment was that caused an alteration to the pump mechanism, from that moment on it is not working properly, and this causes a domino effect. Though it is not something that can be felt, the nutrients are no longer flowing through the disc properly, and the disc is not as healthy as it once was; slowly it begins to degrade. When the disc degrades it becomes weaker and more susceptible to bulges and herniations.

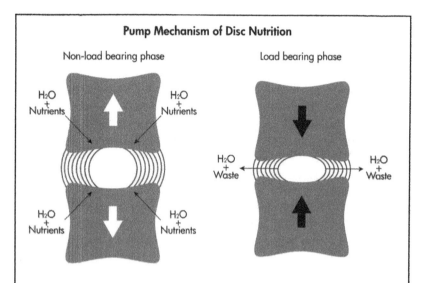

Pump Mechanism of Disc Nutrition

Non-load bearing phase | Load bearing phase

H_2O + Nutrients | H_2O + Nutrients | H_2O + Waste | H_2O + Waste | H_2O + Nutrients | H_2O + Nutrients

The pump mechanism of disc nutrition is driven by movement. When our bodies move, the pump mechanism alternates between compressing and relaxing pressure on the disc. During the non-load bearing phase, water and nutrients get pumped into the disc and during the load bearing phase, water and waste gets pumped out. When this pump mechanism fails, biochemical changes occur to the disc that lead to deterioration and increased susceptibility to disc bulges, herniations, and degenerative disc disease.

If you take a jelly donut and squeeze it between two plates, when the pressure becomes too great, the jelly will begin to squeeze through the donut (see diagram on next page). Similarly, in a disc bulge, the jelly pushes out against the cartilage which is holding the jelly in, causing a bulge, but the jelly is still contained; it has not ruptured. The bulging cartilage can hit the spinal cord or the nerve roots and this may cause pain, numbness, tingling, weakness, burning pain, electric pain, or even a feeling as if you have been stabbed by a hot poker. Sometimes the pain will radiate from the low back into the buttocks or the hips, or cause sciatica or shooting pain down the leg. If the disc bulge is in the neck, it can cause similar pains in the neck, shoulder, arms, hands, or fingers.

If the jelly in the spine is pressed too hard it can actually tear through the cartilage wall; this is known as a "herniation." The type of hernia that people have often heard of is an *inguinal hernia,* where the intestines tear through the groin muscles. In the spine, the jelly tears through the cartilage that contains it and pushes out against the nerves, causing excruciating pain and increasing many of the symptoms just described with the disc bulge.

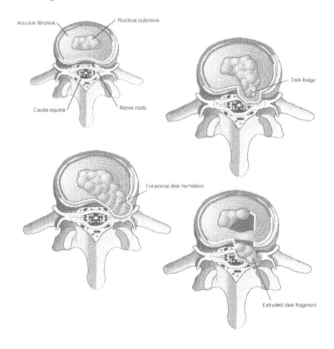

Degenerative Disc Disease

Disc bulges and herniations will often lead to degenerative disc disease. Once a disc is injured the pump mechanism no longer functions properly, and over time the disc will start to desiccate. Desiccation is the loss of nutrients, or dehydration within the disc. Over time, the nutrients seep out and there is nothing pumping the nutrients back into the disc and the disc will start to become more acidic. Over months and years, the disc starts to break down, and one gets degenerative disc disease. It is called that because the bony portions around the disc degenerate and become more calcified or arthritic. The disc(s) starts to dissolve and compress, a significant loss of height will occur, and eventually the disc(s) will become so compressed that the nerves will get pinched.

Spinal Stenosis

Stenosis simply means "narrowing." There are different types of narrowing:

Central Canal Stenosis: This is when the bony canal that surrounds the spinal cord, also known as the central canal, is narrowed. When central canal stenosis is due to a bulge or a herniation, the jelly or cartilage sticks out far enough into the central canal to cause narrowing of that canal. When the cause is a herniation or bulge, it is treatable without surgery.

Lateral Canal or Foraminal Stenosis: This happens when the jelly or cartilage pushes out into the side canals, or lateral canals, where the nerves are, sometimes causing narrowing enough to pinch the nerves. This too is something that can be treated without surgery.

Another type of narrowing, also called **Lateral Canal** or **Foraminal Stenosis,** occurs when arthritis or bone spurs start to form in the side canals. This will often happen in addition to the narrowing caused by a bulge or herniation. Again, this can also be treated without surgery.

The only type of spinal stenosis that spinal decompression therapy is unable to help is a form of central canal stenosis where the narrowing is specifically due to bony calcifications. This occurs more often in women in their 80s or 90s. This is very difficult to treat, and often will result in spinal surgery. Ninety-eight percent of the cases I have in my practice do not have this form of stenosis. Most of the cases I encounter with my patients have one of the other types of stenosis, all of which spinal decompression can help significantly.

3

The Typical Medical Model for Back Pain

Phase 1: *Anti-Inflammatories and Pain Medication*

As mentioned in my introduction, the early phases of traditional medical care all focus on treating symptoms. Whether you are given pain medication, exercises, injections, or sometimes even surgery, the primary concern in standard medical practice is to provide pain relief. You may ask, "So, what's wrong with that? I want pain relief. I NEED pain relief!" Of course you need pain relief. But if the reason you are suffering is due to a disc bulge or herniation, and pain relief is all you are provided, then the relief you feel today will only be temporary. What's worse is that if we don't take care of the cause of your pain, the source of it will continue to do damage to your body and become a bigger and potentially permanent problem.

Phase 2: *Physical Therapy*

Traditional and complementary medicines such as physical therapy, chiropractic manipulative therapy, acupuncture, massage therapy, traction, inversion and specific rehabilitation exercises will sometimes help with the pain caused by a minor disc bulge or herniation. This is because all of these modalities help reduce inflammation and inflammation causes pain. This does not mean, however, that the herniation has receded, or that the pump mechanism is working properly and the problem is resolved. Even if these treatments are helpful it is often just a matter of time before the pain returns, especially when you make a sudden or incorrect movement, or lift something heavy that affects the disc. Additional pressure may cause the disc to bulge or herniate even further, causing even more damage.

Phase 3: *Spinal Epidural Injections, A.K.A. Cortisone Shots*

The second phase of the standard medical model of treating disc problems, as we've said, is to give patients injections. These injections are provided to reduce inflammation, thereby alleviating pain. This is done by an injection of cortisone into the spine at the location of the affected discs. Cortisone is a steroid which is a powerful anti-inflammatory agent. This injection is often guided by fluoroscopy, an imaging technique that uses real-time x-rays to guide the injection. The procedure is conducted under a local anesthetic while the patient is awake. The patient lies on his or her stomach and the doctor first injects a dye to confirm that he or she is in the proper location where the cortisone is needed. The doctor then injects the cortisone. The procedure takes about twenty minutes and is often conducted in an out-patient facility.

The Mayo Clinic provides the following list of risks involved in receiving cortisone shots:

- Death of nearby bone (osteonecrosis)
- Joint infection
- Nerve damage
- Thinning of skin and soft tissue around injection site
- Temporary flare of pain and inflammation in the joint
- Tendon weakening or rupture
- Thinning of nearby bone (osteoporosis)
- Whitening or lightening of the skin around the injection site.

The number of allowable cortisone injections is limited due to the potential deterioration of the cartilage in a joint. Patients should not be given multiple shots within six weeks. They also should not have more than three to four cortisone shots within a one year time span.[1]

Another drawback of such injections is that it can cause scar tissue to form, and the resulting scar tissue can then stiffen the affected area, possibly reducing both the flexibility of the muscles and the chances of healing.

And, as mentioned previously, for some patients the cortisone shot is ineffective. There is no way to know whether the shot will help prior to having it, so a patient basically has to take their chance with this procedure.

Cortisone injections do have validity within the modalities of treatment. When a patient is in significant pain, it may be worth a shot (pun intended) to attempt to provide pain relief. The patient needs to understand, however, that the shots are merely a Band-Aid and do not fix the problem. Therefore they should seek further treatment in addition to the injection. I commonly see patients who believed the injection had cured their condition, only to wind up with a more severe injury. This happens because cortisone injections provide a false belief that the problem is gone, which can cause patients to resume activities that can aggravate their conditions.

Phase 4: *Spinal Surgery*

Surgery is sometimes necessary, but should not be considered unless it is the absolute last resort. In the standard medical model, when presenting with a lower back problem such as a herniated or ruptured disc, where conventional therapies such as medication, physical therapy, and epidural injections did not work, the only option left (too many people believe) is back surgery.

The number one reason that people have back surgery has been shown to be having had a previous back surgery. In fact, WebMD published an article on back surgery originally printed in Good Housekeeping Magazine which read:

Back surgeries can fail for a devastatingly simple reason: The operation was not the right treatment, because the surgeon never pinpointed the source of the pain. As a result, patients may be just as miserable as they were before - or worse off - and a desperate number choose to try again.[2]

Types of Back Surgeries

Here are the predominant types of surgical procedures that are used to treat back and neck pain:

Microdiscectomy
This procedure is the least invasive and most common of the three main spinal surgeries. It is done using an operating microscope or loupe for magnification. Minimally invasive laser spine surgery also uses the same type of procedure but that form of surgery is done with a laser, and microdiscectomy is done with a scalpel. In this type of surgery, the surgeon shaves off a piece of the disc that is sticking out or pressing against the spinal cord or nerve roots. He removes a portion of the *nucleus pulposus* (the inner jelly-like substance that cushions the discs) or cartilage that is sticking into the nerve root or the peripheral nerves.

Microdiscectomy does not improve the functioning of the disc and the procedure carries with it the question of long-term continued degeneration of the spinal disc and the potential necessity for further operations. In addition, by shaving off the offending portion of the *nucleus pulposus* that is pressing on a nerve, the surgeon is reducing the overall size and weight of the jelly, leaving a reduction in the spine's ability to function as a shock absorber.

While the patient may wake up from surgery without shooting pain down their leg, the problem is that they have not addressed the faulty pump mechanism. Consider this analogy: you have a nice green plant and one of the leaves has turned half brown and wilted. If you rip off that dead piece of the leaf, did you fix the problem? No; the plant is not healthy, and the same is true of the disc. Nothing has fixed the pump mechanism, leaving the disc susceptible to re-injury. This is why so many spinal surgery patients wind up having a second surgery.

Laminectomy
The *lamina* is a portion of bone in the back part of the vertebrae which goes up to the side and back of the spinal cord. *Ectomy* means something is being taken out. Therefore a *laminectomy* is surgery where they cut through the lamina and take a portion of it out. This provides more space in the spinal canal for the cord and nerves.

When performing a laminectomy, the surgeon cuts in to the back in order to reach the spinal canal and is then able to get to the compressed nerve. He removes any bone spurs or areas of calcification that are pressing on the nerves. Laminectomies are the most commonly performed back surgeries to treat spinal stenosis where space in the spine is compromised by either disc material or extra bone growth (i.e. arthritis).

Laminectomies increase the space in the spinal canal: however, this does not particularly solve the problem of pressure on the disc, and further degeneration often happens after the surgery. In addition, scar tissue from the surgery sometimes encroaches on the canal, causing problems similar to the initial condition.

Spinal Fusion Surgery

The third type of back surgery is called a *spinal fusion* surgery. This is the most expensive type of surgery done today. **There is no other type of surgery that makes more money for a hospital than spinal fusion surgery and yet the statistics on the outcome of this particular surgery are staggeringly poor.**[3]

Spinal fusion surgery places metal plates, rods, and screws in and around two or more vertebrae. This fuses the vertebrae together so they cannot move. The problem is that the spine has to move in order to get nutrition into the disc, as previously explained with regards to the pump mechanism.

When spinal fusion surgery fuses everything together, pumping can no longer take place. What ends up happening over time is that the spine ends up fusing completely due to immobility. What starts off as immobilizing one area of the spine ends up immobilizing, or severely limiting, the section above and below the area fused, often creating even more pain than the original problem.

Researchers reviewed records from 1,450 patients in the Ohio Bureau of Workers' Compensation database who had diagnoses of disc degeneration, disc herniation, or radiculopathy, a nerve condition that causes tingling and weakness of the limbs. Half of the patients had surgery to fuse two or more vertebrae in hopes of curing low back pain. The other half had no surgery, even though they had comparable diagnoses.

*After two years, only 26 percent of those who had surgery had actually returned to work. That translates to a resounding 74% failure rate! It also suggests that you have **a 257%** better chance of returning to work IF YOU AVOID SURGERY in the first place!*

That's because 67 percent of patients who had the same exact diagnosis, but DIDN'T get surgery, DID return to work.[4]

Spinal Fusion Surgery due to Spondylolisthesis

When a **vertebrae** slips forward or backward onto the vertebrae above or below it, the condition is known as *spondylolisthesis*. The severity of the slipped vertebrae is measured by degrees or grades. For example:

Slippage is graded I through IV:

Grade I - 1 percent to 25 percent slip.
Grade II - 26 percent to 50 percent slip.
Grade III - 51 percent to 75 percent slip.
Grade IV - 76 percent to 100 percent slip.

The only time I find spinal fusion surgery to be warranted is in spondylolisthesis cases of grade three or four, and for some cases, grade two. At a grade two or three the slipping bones become unstable and the vertebrae are displaced either forward or backward in relation to the vertebrae below. In my opinion, spinal fusion should not be used in any instance where someone just has a herniated disc at one or two levels.

The problem with surgery is that even when they say the

surgery is "successful," the definition of success is vague or minimal.

While surgeons may claim that the operation was successful, the main question is whether the patient boasts the same success; i.e., has their pain been eliminated?

Success in surgery is when the pain is released. However, the number of cases that walk into my office that have had surgery in their back and have had the pain return in six months, a year, or even three years, is just staggering.

Why does this happen?

Reason number one: If the pump mechanism hasn't been addressed, the disc remains unhealthy. Just because the surgeon took the pressure off the nerve does not mean that the core problem was resolved. Also, after the surgery the patient is weaker within the areas that have been operated on.

Reason number two: When you have any type of back surgery, whether it is a microdiscectomy, laminectomy, or minimally invasive laser spine surgery in which they just make small incisions, the surgeon has to cut through skin, fat, layers of fascia (connective tissue around muscle), muscle, cartilage, and even bone. In order to get to the target area, there is a lot of maneuvering through body tissue. As mentioned, this will cause scar tissue to form as the body begins to heal itself. Scar tissue is not as strong as the initial cartilage, so it is susceptible to tearing more easily. Sometimes this scar tissue will actually end up pinching a nerve; in some cases this can be as bad, or worse, than the original problem that required the operation to begin with. Very often, surgeons have to perform a second surgery to clear out the scar tissue that occurred as a result of the initial surgery.

It amazes me when a patient comes into my office and says, "I'm having surgery tomorrow." Even after explaining the complications, poor success rate, and lack of necessity for surgery, as well as how spinal decompression can provide true relief without any of the problems, some patients still respond with, "surgery will be faster."

What they do not realize is that recovery from a spinal operation is a big deal. Sometimes there are several days of hospitalization. Then there's the recovery process. After surgery, they have to go through weeks, or possibly even months of physical therapy. Some surgeons do not recommend physical therapy after surgery. This is even worse because the patient doesn't learn how to strengthen their core muscles which are integral in preventing reoccurrence.

The process of recovery from spinal surgery can take just as long as it would have taken for me to treat someone from start to finish. This includes the time I would have spent teaching the patient all of the rehabilitation exercises they would need to strengthen their core after completing spinal decompression therapy.

There are many patients who come into my office because they have been told that they need surgery, and they are looking for another option. Many patients tell me that they know a number of people who have had back surgery and that every one of them is in greater pain today. These patients say there's no way that they are going under the knife.

Spine Surgery: Analysis of 942 consecutive patients
Spine J, 2012(1):22-34

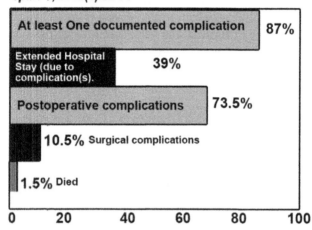

In the 70's, 80's, and 90's, when a surgeon told a patient they needed back surgery, the patient had back surgery. The patient would not second-guess the surgeon. These days, when the surgeon tells a patient they need surgery, the first thing the patient tends to do is "Google" it. They come across hundreds, if not thousands of different accounts of patients who write, "I curse the day I had the back surgery," "I wish I'd never done it," "I wish I had never received that advice," "I wish I tried extra 'x' or 'y' first," "I was in a rush, I listened, and I made a big mistake."

On the opposite end of the spectrum I have had patients that I could not help, and surgery was the right choice for them. Because it was the right choice, it was able to help them. I've had patients who needed back surgery to remove a tumor, patients with true instability in their spine, and patients who had a neurological emergency causing them to need surgery. These are the times when surgery is the appropriate action.

Reasons why surgery can be indicated include: neurological deficits such as losing control of one's bowels or bladder; saddle anesthesia (a complete numbing of the buttocks area); and in cases of progressive weakness where the extremities are rapidly getting weaker.

For the most part, surgery can and should be avoided. Even for patients who have MRIs indicating serious back conditions, spinal decompression therapy can often provide the necessary resolution of the issue.

To ensure whether surgery is absolutely necessary, I perform a comprehensive orthopedic exam and test patients for neurologic symptoms. Too often patients come into my office after having been to physical therapists and after having failed cortisone injections, and now they have been told that surgery is their only option. However, neurologically, even if they are experiencing a ten out of ten on the pain scale, or as patients say a 'fifteen out of ten,' or an 'off the charts' degree of pain, if they do not have weakness or reflex loss or any change in bowel or bladder control, there is no reason for them to have surgery.

Sources

1. "Cortisone Shots." *Risks*. The Mayo Clinic, 17 Apr. 2014.

2. Gerber Hope, Toni, Ince, Susan. "The Truth About Back Surgery." *Good Housekeeping*. 10, Oct. 2011.

3. Walderman, Peter, and David Armstrong. "Doctors Getting Rich With Fusion Surgery Debunked by Studies." *Bloomberg.com*. BloombergBusiness, 30 Dec. 2010.

4. Nguyen, Randolph TH, DC, J. Talmage, P. Succop, and R. Travis. *"Long-Term Outcomes of Lumbar Fusion Among Workers' Compensation Subjects: An Historical Cohort Study."* Long-Term Outcomes of Lumbar Fusion Among Workers' Compensation Subjects: An Historical Cohort Study. Chiropractic Resource Organization, 23 Oct. 2010.

4

Spinal Decompression

What Is Spinal Decompression?

When a disc is herniated, bulging, or compressed, it can pinch the spinal cord or the spinal nerves, causing pain. Non-surgical spinal decompression therapy is a technique utilizing specific machines to apply a distraction force to the targeted compressed, bulging, or herniated disc(s). It is the only technique that creates a negative pressure inside the disc which forces the bulge or herniation to retract off the nerve or spinal cord. This negative pressure causes a "vacuum effect" which sucks the jelly, water, and nutrients back into the disc where they belong.

The following before and after MRI images are from one of my patients.

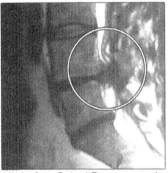 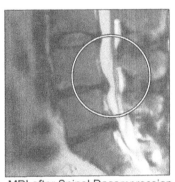

MRI before Spinal Decompression   MRI after Spinal Decompression

The repetitive nature of the treatment retrains the disc to pump properly, thereby restoring the pump mechanism of disc nutrition. The disc itself is active tissue that contains significant mechanisms for self-repair.[1] This technique holds true whether we are working on a disc(s) in the back or disc(s) in the neck.

Consider this: If I were to ask you to stick out your arm,

45

and I grabbed your hand and pulled, your immediate reaction would be to pull back and resist my pull. That is a natural reflex that our body has; when muscles are pulled, their reaction is to immediately resist.

Your spine is surrounded by layers and layers of strong muscles. If I laid you down on a traction table and I yanked your back, what would happen? All the surrounding muscles of your spine would reflexively resist and protect your spine, and I would therefore not be able to accomplish much deep down in the disc due to your muscles resisting. That is why traction is usually ineffective for treating disc bulges and herniations.

In spinal decompression therapy, a different technique is applied that allows the body to adjust comfortably to the treatment so that it can be effective. This is how it works: there is a special belt that goes just above a patient's hips but below the level of the discs we want to treat, and another belt that gets attached above the level of the discs we want to treat. The lower belt is connected to a very sensitive computer, while the upper belt is kept firmly in place by a connection to the table. Spinal decompression can be accomplished with the patient either lying flat on their stomach, or lying on their back with soft bolsters raising and supporting their knees. Ninety-nine percent of patients are more comfortable having the treatment while lying on their back. The computer regulates how hard, how fast, and how long each treatment cycle is. The treatment table has different segments, allowing a portion of the table to open up underneath the patient's body during the treatment. This helps reduce friction.

The computer will start gently pulling the belts apart. During this time, the segments of the table will move in conjunction with the pull. After a few pounds of tension the machine will hold the pull in place, allowing the patient's body and muscles to adapt to that level of resistance. (We are not yanking it, we are gently stretching it, and allowing it to adjust comfortably.) After fifteen seconds the machine will then increase several more pounds and then stop at that increased level, allowing the patient's body to get used to the new level of pull. This action will be repeated several times over a couple of minutes until the machine reaches the predetermined treatment weight that the doctor has set into the spinal decompression computer. This beginning process is essential so that your body doesn't just initially react to the machine like it would to traction where all of your muscles would automatically resist. Once the top weight has been reached, the machine will hold at that weight for thirty to forty five seconds. Next, the machine will relax to half the top weight, which allows the table segments below the patient to start to return toward each other. After fifteen to twenty seconds at that lower level, the machine goes back to pulling at the top weight.

The machine will then repeat this cycle of pulling and relaxing, pulling and relaxing, for between twenty to thirty minutes. This allows all of the surrounding spine musculature to shut off and relax and helps initiate a negative pressure inside the disc. This negative pressure creates the suction (or vacuum) effect that causes water, nutrients, and disc material to be sucked back toward the center of the disc and off the nerves as mentioned previously. Anti-inflammatories, pain medications, physical therapy, traction, inversion, massage, acupuncture, chiropractic manipulation, cortisone shots, and surgery cannot do this. Only spinal decompression therapy can create the negative pressure necessary to suck a bulge or herniation back into the disc.

Spinal decompression therapy is extremely comfortable

and relaxing. Most patients really enjoy the treatment, and many even fall asleep.

Spinal Decompression vs Traction

Similar to testing air pressure in tires, scientists can test different types of pressure put on discs while a patient is sitting, standing, lying flat[2], while in traction[3], or while in spinal decompression therapy. Pressures between the discs are measured in millimeters of mercury (mm Hg). Millimeters of mercury are also used when measuring blood pressure. While standing there is an average of 100mm Hg of pressure on the lumbar discs. When lying down that pressure reduces to 75mm Hg. While in traction, pressure can be reduced as low as 40mm Hg. Spinal decompression, on the other hand is the only known therapy able to achieve a negative pressure, which has been noted to reach as low as -160mm Hg[4]. This negative pressure is what causes the vacuum effect that sucks the nutrients and the herniated jelly-like material back into the discs.

A study was conducted in 1997 comparing traction to spinal decompression therapy. It concluded that there were no benefits when using traction for herniated discs, while spinal decompression therapy showed "good" to "excellent" results for nearly all patients with herniated discs.[5]

Even when patients have lateral canal or foraminal stenosis where there is a bone spur in addition to a bulge or herniation pushing on the nerve, spinal decompression therapy helps because as we draw the water, nutrients, and disc material back to the center of the disc, it increases the height of the disc (picture a jack pumping up the tire of a car). This increased height creates more space in the canal where the nerves reside, so even if there was a nerve previously pinched by a bone spur, there is now enough space for the nerve to move freely.

Remember that almost everybody over the age of thirty-five has some bone spurs or arthritis. Most people in this age group do not feel pain because the nerve is not being pinched. What causes pain is when there is not enough space for the bone spur and it compresses a nerve. We're not going in there surgically and shaving off any bone spurs; we're just creating space for them.

Non-Surgical Spinal Decompression Decreases Low Back Pain

In 2010, a study was conducted on 30 adults with an average age of 65 who had a lumbar disc herniation. During a 6 week treatment protocol of non-surgical spinal decompression their pain levels decreased from a 6.2 to a 1.6 level of pain. In addition, the disc height measured via CT scans increased during treatment which was directly correlated to the reduction of pain.[6]

Not only does spinal decompression therapy cause this negative pressure that sucks water, nutrients, and disc material back in, but this repetition and pumping that the machine does recreates the pump mechanism. By doing this for many treatments over several weeks, we are able to re-teach the body's natural pump mechanism how to function properly. I often hear my patients tell me that even months after treatment has been completed, they continue to feel even better and better.

Studies Show

A four-year, multi-center follow-up study on the lasting effects of vertebral axial decompression (spinal decompression) reported "remarkable levels of sustained relief in 23 back pain patients." All patients had undergone several types of treatment before receiving this spinal decompression therapy.[7] Prior to this treatment their pain levels were considered severe with patients rating the pain a 7.41 out of a possible scale of 8 being the most severe. Immediately after treatment, the pain levels were being reported at a level of 3.41 – a significant difference. And four years later their pain relief continued to improve as shown by the following statistics:

- 91% were able to resume their normal daily activities.
- 86% showed a 50% or better pain reduction.
- Employment status increased by 40% among those previously out of work due to back pain.
- 87% were either working or were retired without having back pain as the cause of retirement.
- 52% of respondents reported a pain level of zero.
- Average pain levels further reduced to 1.57.[8]

For a list of all the relevant spinal decompression studies, please go to my website: www.SpinalDecompressionResearch.com

You Must Be a Candidate for This Treatment

Not everyone is a candidate for spinal decompression therapy. In my office, I have four specific criteria my patients must meet prior to my accepting them for treatment.

Number One: The patient must have an MRI showing at least one of the signs of compression which can be corrected by spinal decompression. Once I view the images, I will know if spinal decompression is the right course of action for the patient. In addition, the patient must not have any of the following conditions that would be contraindicated to spinal decompression: a spinal tumor; active cancer; severe osteoporosis; recent fractures; a grade of spondylolisthesis (bone slippage) too unstable for the procedure; or, in most cases of a previous spinal fusion surgery.

Number Two: Neurologically, everything has to correlate to the MRI, but it cannot be so bad that I cannot fix it. In other words, every bit of information I have received from the patient - from their intake, the detailed history I took from them, and my orthopedic and neurological exam - has to come together to show me that the pain they are experiencing correlates to what I see on their MRI. It also cannot be so bad that I think it is an emergency that requires immediate surgery. (These true neurological emergencies were described in a previous chapter.) I can almost always rid a patient of their pain. There is a bit more uncertainty involved in cases where the patient is suffering from **constant** numbness, tingling, and/or weakness. If a patient's foot is numb, but the numbness comes and goes, then I can be confident that we can still get feeling back into that foot. It is only when the numbness, tingling, or weakness has been constant for several months or years that there is no way for me or any other doctor to know whether that nerve can be recovered. Whether a surgeon surgically takes the pressure off the nerve or if I, utilizing spinal decompression therapy, naturally take the pressure off the nerve, the nerve has been damaged and it will take time to regenerate. It can take up to one and a half years for a nerve to regenerate, and if one and a half years after surgery, or my treatment, the patient still has numbness, tingling, or weakness, it will in all likelihood be permanent. Unfortunately there is no test or any other way to know before someone has surgery or goes through spinal decompression therapy whether the nerve is already permanently damaged.

I want my patients to have realistic and rational expectations. Even in cases where the patient has had chronic pain for thirty years, I am highly confident that I can eliminate their pain. It is only with the longstanding **constant** numbness, tingling, or weakness that I cannot be as certain. That being said, the pressure still has to be removed, because the process is degenerative and will only continue to get worse.

Number Three: A patient must understand that spinal decompression therapy is an investment in both a.) Time and b.) Money.

3A.) Time: Unlike a typical neck or back strain where it might just take a handful of sessions to get a patient out of pain, with spinal decompression therapy we are trying to both get them out of pain and fix the problem. The typical course of treatment consists of twenty to forty sessions. The number of treatments is determined by these factors:

- Age of the patient
- Number of discs affected
- Severity of the compression, bulge(s), or herniation(s)
- Degree of degeneration

- Degree of symptoms
- Previous history of back or neck surgery

We treat our patients between three and four times a week. Why so much? If I put a patient on the machine for one session and then I don't see them again for a whole week, a myriad of things may happen between that initial treatment and their next which could render the first treatment less effective. For example: once the patient gets off the machine, gravity reasserts itself and puts pressure back on the disc. Once the patient leaves my office they can drive over a pothole on the way home, or they may wind up lifting heavy loads of laundry, or lifting their kids, etc. Any number of other events can begin to undo the effects of treatment. This is why we need to treat so regularly; spinal decompression therapy is a cumulative treatment. Each visit is approximately thirty minutes, and in most cases the patient spends twenty to twenty five of those minutes on the machine. The remaining time is spent setting up the patient and taking them off the machine. Later on in the course of treatment they are taught core strengthening exercises and specific stretches.

3B.) Money:
Spinal decompression therapy is currently not covered by any health insurance companies or Medicare, and I will explain my theories on why not at the end of this section. Therefore a patient must understand that there is currently no reimbursement for spinal decompression services.

Regardless of your financial situation, we pride ourselves on providing several different affordable payment plans so that anyone can afford this treatment.

Number Four: I only choose patients who I think are going to be compliant for my program. It is your back or neck, but it is also my reputation. This treatment requires a commitment. Obviously I cannot get you better without you showing up for your appointments, but it is more than just that. I have a specific protocol which my patients must follow to get the best results.

Spinal Decompression Protocol

The neck and back protocol are identical, except that there is no brace for the neck.

A.) Disc Distractor Brace/Belt: This brace is designed specifically for disc problems in the low back. It reduces pressure on the discs, but cannot cause negative pressure like the spinal decompression machine. Instead of gravity just pulling right back on the disc when you get off the machine, if you put the brace on right away it will help reduce the pressure of gravity.

Most patients find the brace extremely comfortable and helpful. It is mandatory to wear the brace for two hours following treatment in order to reinforce the progress that was just made. After that, it is no longer mandatory, but for those patients who are still having pain it is suggested that they wear the brace all day, as long as it is comfortable. Patients who have pain at night are allowed to sleep with the brace, but that is not necessary for those patients who do not experience pain during those hours. The brace has a convenient slot in the back for an ice or heat pack, which brings us to B.

B.) Ice Therapy: Ice is part of my protocol because of the significant relief it provides to patients who are having pain. (This is true for back and neck disc problems as well as other chronic pain conditions). Ice might be considered a supplement to, or even a replacement for, cortisone injections. Over the years I have become a strong proponent of "ice therapy" as a means of pain and inflammation reduction. Inflammation causes pain. Ice reduces inflammation. Obviously applying ice does not address the underlying compression issues, but it does address, to some degree, the immediate problem of pain.

If there is something pressing on the spinal cord or nerve and the body is inflamed, over-the-counter anti-inflammatory drugs can work by getting the inflammation under control. This can alleviate the immediate pain, but it does not fix the underlying problem.

Heat can sometimes calm down a strained muscle, but when a disc is herniated and has acute inflammation there is already a lot of blood in the area trying to heal the condition. Adding heat causes more blood to rush to the area, causing more swelling, which may increase the pain. Sometimes a patient will put a hot pack on their lower back and then find that they simply cannot get back up. This is because they have put heat on an already inflamed area, making the situation worse.

If a patient is not sure whether to use heat or ice, the answer is to always use ice. Ice will never hurt you as long as you use it in specific increments: twenty minutes on, forty minutes off (back in the freezer). Do not leave it on for more than twenty minutes at a time. If you ice for too long you will encounter something called the *Huntington Reflex*. This is a phenomenon where after twenty minutes of icing, capillaries will re-open and blood will rush back to the area being iced. This would then cause the same effect we just described with the hot pack. So remember - ice is your first choice, but limit the use to 20 minutes on, 40 minutes off, and repeat the cycle as often as you can.

It is very important to note that when a patient utilizes ice they should never apply it directly to their skin; it must always be used over a piece of clothing or under a towel, as it can burn the skin otherwise.

C.) Nutritional supplementation: In 2007, I attended a spinal decompression conference and heard two of my colleagues raving that their results were better when they gave patients two specific supplements. I immediately started using them with my own patients and have seen the results for spinal decompression get even better. The first one is a high grade fish oil. This is good for reducing pain and inflammation, as well as providing a host of other health benefits. The other is Arthrosoothe by Designs For Health. This is a blend of glucosamine, hyaluronic acid, MSM, collagen, and a bunch of anti-inflammatory herbs. Due to the degeneration that ensues after patients have disc bulges or herniations, they lose some of these important nutrients inside the disc. We compensate for this by giving them these particular oral supplements. Then, when we cause the vacuum effect with spinal decompression therapy, it pulls those nutrients back into the disc. Since using Arthrosoothe, I have seen astounding results in my office. Patients who had been told that knee or hip replacements were their only option wound up getting relief when nothing else helped. Not a week goes by without some patient telling me that their shoulder, knee, ankle, wrist, or hand pain went away. I know their relief is due to the effects of the Athrosoothe product because these were areas I did not treat, and these patients had not taken any other new medications.

D.) Core strengthening rehabilitation program:
Numerous studies show that back and neck pain is

extremely recurrent. Once you have it, and a particular episode seems to be resolved, invariably the pain continues to come back.

With disc bulges and herniations, degenerative disc disease, and spinal stenosis, the percentage of recurrence is off the charts. Without spinal decompression therapy, three things will unequivocally happen:

- The episodes of back or neck pain will reoccur more often
- They will start to last longer
- They will become more severe

Once we fix the pump mechanism, and get the pressure off the nerves, we will introduce a set of core strengthening exercises and stretches. As long as patients do these stretches and exercises, the chance of recurrence precipitously drops. A number of the previously mentioned exercises will be talked about and demonstrated in chapter six.

There are muscles in our core called local stabilizing muscles. These include the transverse abdominus, internal obliques, diaphragm, pelvic floor, and multifidi muscles. They are supposed to engage and fire when we do almost anything: when we talk, when we walk, and when we move. For most people, as they get older, these muscles become weak and inhibited and stop working properly. When this happens, our much bigger global mobilizing muscles, like our large erector spinae muscles in our neck and back, have to pick up the slack and are constantly working. Eventually, these muscles fatigue and leave our bodies extremely susceptible to injury or re-injury. The core strengthening exercises target these smaller local stabilizing posture muscles to "wake them up" and help strengthen them, rebalancing the system.

Maintenance

Once the patient completes their course of spinal decompression therapy in my office, I discharge them. **The greatest chance of setback or relapse occurs within the first year following spinal decompression therapy.** It usually takes about a full year for layers of cartilage to completely heal now that the pump mechanism is working properly. During that year I suggest, but do not make it mandatory, that patients come in once a month for a spinal decompression treatment. The older the patient is the more necessary that becomes, because many of them have very severe degenerative disc disease and even though I've created some space for the nerves, if left untreated indefinitely, eventually gravity will pull the discs back down. Even in cases where my patients' pain does reoccur several years after treatment, it almost never takes more than a handful of additional treatments to get them back on track.

Which Spinal Decompression Machine is the Best?

This is a question I often get from patients since there are almost a dozen different manufactures. They all utilize very similar technology to accomplish the same affect, which is to create negative pressure in the disc(s). My practice now has 6 spinal decompression machines, all by the same manufacturer.

When I first started to offer spinal decompression therapy, I learned the technique from the rep who sold the machine. He spent four hours teaching me how the machine works. For many doctors this is the extent of their instruction. Most of them use a cookie-cutter approach based on this insufficient training. I was so impressed with the potential of this technology that I underwent extensive additional training to become an expert in the treatment of serious disc conditions utilizing spinal decompression therapy. I have subsequently treated thousands of patients using this method. It is important to choose a doctor with extensive experience as well as superior knowledge of this machinery and how to use it to properly treat a patient. It is more important that you select a doctor you trust than you select one by the type of machine they use.

My theory on why spinal decompression therapy is not covered by insurance:

I would like to answer the commonly asked question, "If spinal decompression therapy is so great, why isn't it covered by insurance?"

You've probably noticed that your coverage changes when your policy renews and often services that you previously had are no longer part of the plan. This can be frustrating, especially when insurance companies cover procedures like cortisone injections even though studies have shown that these procedures are temporary fixes and do not prevent nor lessen a patient's chance of having surgery. Spinal decompression, on the other hand, is far less expensive, far more effective, and a real solution to many disc problems. Surgery *is* often covered by insurance, even though it is extremely expensive, usually a temporary and incomplete fix, and most often *not* a true solution for the core problem.

So why is spinal decompression denied on insurance claims? Because insurance companies consider the procedure 'experimental.' The truth is, spinal decompression is not experimental. It has been used for over 20 years with many studies proving its success rate and validity. (www.SpinalDecompressionResearch.com)

Every drug you've ever taken is FDA "approved." The spinal decompression therapy machinery is FDA "cleared." (Drugs get FDA approved, machinery can only get FDA cleared.) The way drugs get approved is through what are called double-blind placebo/control studies. Any drug you've ever taken, whether it is Tylenol or Vicodin or anything in between, has been given to two groups of people. Let's call them Group A and Group B. The reason they're called double-blind studies is that neither group A nor B will know whether they're getting the real drug or a placebo (a sugar pill) that looks just like the real drug. The doctor is also unaware whether the patient is receiving the real pill or the placebo, eliminating the chance that the patient will be subliminally influenced by what the doctor knows. The reason this is such an effective study is due to something called "the placebo effect": let's say 25% of Group A gets better, and 70% of Group B gets better. Well, in Group A, 25% of the patients improved because of the placebo effect; they improved simply because they took a pill thinking it would help them, and that was enough to improve their symptoms. The 70% improvement experienced by Group B, however, is statistically significant and it shows that the drug actually works. Assuming the drug proves safe and is not toxic in any way, the drug will get approved. Unfortunately when it comes to physical medicine like spinal decompression therapy, you cannot have a double-blind placebo/control study; there is no way the patient can be unaware whether or not they have had the treatment - they have clearly either been on the therapy table or they have not. No matter how good follow-up studies showing pre-and-post MRI imaging are, and no matter how many studies are performed showing that an extraordinarily high rate of patients still do not have pain four or five years after finishing the treatment, the insurance companies are still not covering it. A good example of a procedure that works well, but is not covered by insurance, is Lasik surgery. After having Lasik surgery performed on your eyes, you can go from needing glasses to not needing glasses - it works great; insurance doesn't cover it.

Spinal fusion surgeries make more money for doctors and hospitals than any other procedure performed on the entire body, yet it has one of the worst outcomes of any procedure performed today.[9]

One of the doctors I treated works at a prestigious hospital and has overseen hundreds if not thousands of spinal surgeries. He had chronic back pain for years before I helped him with spinal decompression therapy. He told me that he's heard his physician colleagues joke that "The only back surgery not needed was the first one."

Another medical doctor, who I had treated successfully with spinal decompression therapy, introduced me to the pain management doctor who had given him several epidural (cortisone) injections. This pain management doctor came to my office and was very impressed with spinal decompression therapy. I was excited at the prospect of the endless amount of referrals I would get from this doctor. In the year and a half following that first meeting, however, less than a handful of referrals came. Recently he volunteered that the reason he had not referred more patients to me was because 98% of his patients are referred to him by neurosurgeons. He is therefore in a bind because the reason the neurosurgeons are sending him their patients is because they cannot get the surgery approved by the insurance company until a patient has had 3 epidural injections. His entire business is dependent upon their referrals. If he referred those patients to me, the neurosurgeons would send their patients elsewhere.

The above examples illustrate my frustration with the medical structure in place that doesn't recognize and embrace the importance of a therapy that can save time, pain, and money from people who are truly suffering. This is one of the reasons I wrote this book. It is my hope to enlighten anyone that is a candidate to receive spinal decompression therapy to try it first, BEFORE surgery.

Sources:

1. Human intervertebral disc: structure and function.
Humzah MD, Soames RW
Anat Rec. 1988 Apr; 220(4):337-56.

2 Nachemson, Alf, MD,PhD, The Load on Lumbar Discs in Different Positions of the Body. *Clinical Orthopaedics.* 45, 107-122, 1996

3. Andersson, G.B., Schultz, A.B., Nachemson, Alf, MD, PhD, Intervertebral Disc Pressures During Traction, *Scandinavian Journal of Rehabilitation Medicine*, Supplement 9:88-91, 1983

4. Ramos, Gustavo, MD, Martin, William, MD, Effects of Vertebral Axial Decompression on Intradiscal Pressure, Journal of Neurosurgery, 81(3), 1994. Study Performed on a VAX-D™ Table.

5. Shealy, C. Norma, MD, PhD, Borgmeyer, Vera, RN, MA, Decompression, Reduction, and Stabilization of the Lumbar Spine: A Cost Effective Treatment for Lumbosacral

Pain. American Journal of Pain Management. Vol. 7, No. 2 April 1997.

6. Apfel, C.C., O.S. Cakmakkaya, W. Martin, C. Richmond, A. Carcario, E. George, M. Schaefer, and JV Pergolizzi. "Result FRestoration of Disk Height through Non-surgical Spinal Decompression Is Associated with Decreased Discogenic Low Back Pain: A Retrospective Cohort Study.ilters." *National Center for Biotechnology Information.* U.S. National Library of Medicine, 8 July 2010. Web.

7., 8. R.H. Odell, MD, PhD and D.A. Boudreau, DO *Anesthesiology News*, Vol. 29, March 2003

9. Walderman, Peter, and David Armstrong. "Doctors Getting Rich With Fusion Surgery Debunked by Studies." *Bloomberg.com.* BloombergBusiness, 30 Dec. 2010.

5

Complementary Therapies to Spinal Decompression

The vast majority of my spinal decompression patients only get spinal decompression therapy and do not receive any of the treatments discussed in this chapter. Once in a while I will incorporate one of these treatments in conjunction because I may deem it helpful or necessary for the patient.

Chiropractic

Chiropractors have been treating disc bulges and herniations for over a hundred years. To this day when a patient with a non-serious bulge or herniation walks into my office, I will often try to at least get them out of pain using chiropractic. I know that I cannot fix the disc or pump mechanism using chiropractic, but if within a week or two they respond to chiropractic therapy, then I show them core strengthening exercises and see how long their relief lasts. If the patient begins to experience reoccurrences very close together, and chiropractic stops being beneficial, or if they're not getting any results in the first place, then I will suggest spinal decompression therapy. You might ask why I wouldn't just put all of my disc patients on spinal decompression therapy in the first place, and the answer is that I would, except for the fact that spinal decompression is not covered by insurance and will often be quite a bit more expensive than chiropractic care. For this reason, I first see if the less time-consuming and more cost-effective therapy will work for them and use spinal decompression as my plan B.

What Does Chiropractic Do?

Each vertebrae in the spine is cushioned by a disc. Each segment also has two joints, or facets that allow our spine to have motion. Those joints, like the discs, are made out of cartilage. As we've discussed at length in other chapters, cartilage has no blood supply and only gets nutrition through movement. When discs get injured, very often the joints get injured as well. Sometimes the joints get stuck and become restricted in motion. This can be very painful, and it can lead to further dysfunction. As chiropractors we are trained to detect these areas of joint restriction and to manipulate the spine in a very gentle and specific way to help restore motion to those stuck joints.

In 2010 a study was conducted on 85,402 back pain patients in Tennessee. These patients were diagnosed with spinal disc disorders, lower back pain, muscle spasms, joint mobility restrictions, sacroiliac joint sprain/strains, and lumbar spine sprain/strains. Results showed that 61% of the respondents who underwent chiropractic care were "very satisfied" with the results of their treatment, while only 27% of those who underwent traditional medical treatment said they were "very satisfied" with the results of their treatment. In addition, those who underwent chiropractic care incurred 40% less cost than those choosing traditional medical care.[1]

Active Release Techniques (ART)

Active Release Techniques (ART) is a patented, state of the art soft tissue system/movement based massage technique that treats problems with muscles, tendons, ligaments, fascia, and nerves. Headaches, back pain, neck pain, carpal tunnel syndrome, shin splints, shoulder pain, sciatica, plantar fasciitis, and tennis elbow are just a few of the many conditions that can be resolved quickly and permanently with ART. These conditions all have one important thing in common: they are often a result of over-used muscles.

All muscle fibers in the body are parallel. Due to bad posture, constriction of blood flow, and repetitive motion, we get microscopic tears in those fibers, and the parallel strands start to splay haphazardly. The body fills in the gaps in these fibers with a form of scar tissue or "myofascial adhesions."

If one took a brand new paintbrush and painted a wall, the brand new bristles would run very smoothly over the surface being painted. If you were to use that same paintbrush for months, however, over time it would accumulate old paint chips between the bristles would not run as smoothly as before and may even catch in certain places. Our muscles are very similar; they are supposed to glide over one another very smoothly. When we get these myofascial adhesions (or "old paint chips") in the muscles, the fibers start to get stuck, and this lack of motion can cause pain and dysfunction. Sometimes nerves can get caught in these myofascial adhesions and cause radiating pain down the shoulders, arms, hips, buttocks, and legs. This is particularly important in my practice since I see so many disc cases. In ART, the doctor finds an area of the muscle that he feels has adhesions, and presses down on them while the muscle is in its most shortened position. The doctor then shows the patient how to lengthen the muscle. All the while, the doctor keeps the tension over the myofascial adhesions. This strips the fibers and fascia of scar tissue and adhesions and helps return the muscle fibers to their proper parallel positions. It is extremely effective, and often it works in only a few treatments. Sometimes patients will experience a phenomenon called a double crush injury where the nerve can be compressed in two different places. For example, someone can have a herniated disc in their low back, causing sciatica down their leg, and also have myofascial adhesions in their piriformis muscle (which is a deep muscle in the buttocks) which can also pinch the sciatic nerve. If a doctor only fixes one of those areas of compression, the patient's symptoms will not resolve. In cases like that, ART is incredibly effective at clearing up these adhesions and releasing the nerves.

Graston Technique

Graston technique is another soft tissue technique that uses a similar concept to active release techniques. The major difference is that with Graston technique the doctor uses various stainless steel tools, each designed for different body parts, to break up myofascial adhesions. The tools have beveled edges that allow the doctor to feel a vibratory feedback when running this tool over areas of scar tissue. Once we find the adhesions with the tool, we use it to clear them.

I find ART to be more effective on some body parts, and Graston to be more effective on others. As an aside, every major professional sports franchise has a doctor that specializes in both Graston and ART. NFL, MLB, the NBA, the NHL, and PGA tour all have doctors that specialize in ART and Graston techniques.

Low-Level Laser Therapy

Low-level laser therapy (LLLT) is synonymous with cold laser therapy, photobiomodulation, and laser biostimulation. Low-level laser therapy is a safe, non-invasive therapeutic approach that effectively treats chronic pain and trauma. It uses different wavelengths of lasers to penetrate through the skin and into muscles, tendons, and ligaments to stimulate the cells to work faster, speeding up the healing process. This methodology initiates tissue restoration and alleviates painful swelling and inflammation.

How does it work?

Trauma, inflammation, and cellular dysfunction or disorder are the origins of pain and discomfort. Mitochondria, which are called the "power plant" of every cell, supply the lion's share of adenosine triphosphate (ATP), which is the cell's primary source of life-sustaining energy. Mitochondria are organelles which maintain the cycle of cell division, cell duplication and cell growth; therefore they are essential for proper cell function. When cells are affected by injury or age, laser therapy will stimulate the mitochondria to ultimately restore ATP, which aids in healing and reduces stress to the cells.

When cellular balance is restored, pain is alleviated, and the healing process is initiated.

Further, LLLT has the ability to facilitate the robust

development of collagen and cartilage in unstable joints, as well as promote healing of injured tendons and ligaments.

Studies Show:
NSAIDS Do Little for Short-Term Pain

Nonsteroidal anti-inflammatory drugs (NSAIDs) reduce short-term pain associated with knee osteoarthritis only slightly better than a placebo, and long-term use of these agents should be avoided. [2]

In more than 100 double-blind placebo-controlled studies published on the effects of LLLT the results have shown the favorable anti-inflammatory effect of LLLT. Based on the objective, semi-objective, and subjective measurements, after laser and placebo treatments in patients with seropositive rheumatoid arthritis, it was concluded that laser treatment exerts a positive influence on the clinical signs and laboratory parameters of this disease.[3]

In another study, significant positive effects were reported for the relief of neck pain using low level laser therapy (LLLT). [4]

Sources:

1. Capoferri, Donald, DC, DAAMLP, William J. Owens, DC, DAMLP, and Mark Studin, DC, FASBE(C), DAAMLP, DAAPM. "Back Pain: Chiropractic vs. Medical Doctors Who Get Better Results and Who Is More Cost Effective? - US Chiropractic Directory." *Back Pain: Chiropractic vs. Medical Doctors Who Get Better Results and Who Is More Cost Effective? - US Chiropractic Directory*. USCD, 07 Mar. 2015. Web

2. Jan M. Bjordal, British Medical Journal, 2004.

3. Hegedűs B, Viharos L, Gervain M, Gálfi M. The Effect of Low-Level Laser in Knee Osteoarthritis: A Double-Blind, Randomized, Placebo-Controlled Trial.*Photomedicine and Laser Surgery*. 2009;27(4):577-584. doi:10.1089/pho.2008.2297.

4. Roberta T. Chow, Les Barnsley. "Systematic review of the literature of low-level laser therapy (LLLT) in the management of neck pain" *Lasers in Surgery and Medicine*. 2005.

6

In Conclusion

Millions of people suffer with back and neck pain due to bulging or herniated discs, degenerative disc disease, or spinal stenosis. The traditional medical model leads these patients down a path: from medication, to physical therapy, spinal injections, and ultimately to spinal surgery. Spinal decompression therapy should always be explored prior to opting for surgery, because it helps fix the problem for a vast majority of these patients. Bulging and herniated discs can be very painful even when they don't pinch nerves. When they do pinch nerves the pain can radiate to the extremities, as well as cause neurological symptoms such as numbness, tingling, and weakness. The problem is that the discs were injured at some point, and nutrients are no longer being pumped in and out the way they should be. When the pump mechanism isn't working properly, disc bulges and herniations are more likely to occur due to the weakened disc structure. The traditional medical therapies do not address this underlying problem of disc health, but spinal decompression does.

Spinal decompression therapy accomplishes two main goals. First, it creates a negative pressure, causing nutrients and the herniated jelly-material to be sucked back into the center of the discs and off the nerves. Second, the repetitive pumping motion helps repair the pump mechanism so it can function on its own and heal properly.

Before you opt for spinal surgery, you owe it to yourself to see if you are a candidate for non-surgical spinal decompression therapy.

7

Core Strengthening Exercises and Stretches

There are many benefits to core strengthening exercises and stretches. They include:

- Increased muscle strength and endurance
- Increased range of motion
- Decreased pain
- Decreased swelling and inflammation of joints
- Increased coordination and balance
- Increased mobility
- Improved physical well-being and health
- Improved body mechanics and posture
- Decreased stress on other areas of the body
- Increased spinal strength and stability
- Increased joint function and flexibility
- Increased function of the ankle, knee and hip as it relates to balance
- Increased response of the core muscles

This is only a small list of the benefits of core strengthening and stretches.

WARNING: The following exercises and stretches do not fix back and neck pain. They are to be done once you've completed therapy and are out of pain. They will help keep your back and neck in good shape and help prevent further injury.

Someone who has pain in their back or neck should not be doing these exercises or stretches.

Back and Lower Extremity Stretches

#1 Hamstring Stretch

- Starting position: Standing straight with your feet shoulder width apart. Lunge your left foot a full step ahead of your right foot. Keep both your hips squared (facing forward and not twisted to one side).
- Straighten your forward leg completely and rest both of your hands on top of your front knee. Lock the knee so it stays completely straight.
- Slowly bring your chest down toward your front leg. You should start to feel the hamstring stretch on your front leg.
- Hold the stretch for 15 seconds and repeat for the other leg.
- Do not stretch to the point where you feel pain in the hamstring. You just want a gentle stretch.

Repetitions: 3 sets of 15 seconds for each leg.

#1a Hamstring Stretch Alternate Position
(For Those with Balance Issues.)

- Follow the instructions on the previous page. Instead of placing your hands on your front knee, use the wall to brace yourself if you have trouble balancing.

Repetitions: 3 sets of 15 seconds for each leg.

If this stretch reproduces your back pain or causes pain down your leg, stop immediately.

#2 Calf Stretch

- Starting position: Stand in front of a wall. **You must wear shoes for this stretch.**

- Extend your left leg out. Put your toes as high up against the wall as possible while making sure to keep the back edge of your heel against the ground. The toes should be pointing up in the air, resting against the wall and the front leg should remain straight.

- Put your hands on the wall and slowly bring your body forward towards the wall. You should feel the stretch in the calf muscles of your front leg.
- Hold the stretch for 15 seconds and repeat for the other leg.

Repetitions: 3 sets of 15 seconds for each leg.

#3 Glut Stretch

 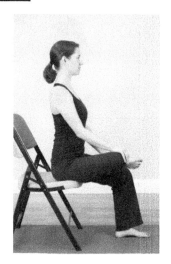

- Starting position: Sit on a chair. Place your right foot on your left knee.

• Lean forward with your head, neck and back in a straight line. You should feel a stretch on the hip and butt muscles on your right side.

You should not feel this in your back at all. If you do, stop until you can do this stretch without feeling it in your back.

• Hold the stretch for 15 seconds. Relax and return to the starting position.

Repetitions: 3 sets of 15 seconds for each leg.

#4 Hip Flexor Stretch

The hip flexors are muscles which attach from the lower levels of your lumbar spine to just below the hip in the front of your thigh.

- First, put a mat or pillow down to serve as a cushion for your knees. Starting position: Put your right knee on the ground and your left leg in a lunge position with your knee bent as seen above.

- Lunge forward while keeping your back straight. Do not allow your knee to extend beyond your toes. You should feel the stretch in the upper thigh of your right leg (the back leg). Hold the stretch for 15 seconds and repeat for the other leg.

Repetitions: 3 sets of 15 seconds each side

#4a Hip Flexor Stretch Alternate Position

- (If you do not feel the stretch in the previous position, while in your forward lunge, lift your right arm overhead and lean towards your left side). Hold the stretch for 15 seconds and repeat for the other leg.

   Repetitions: 3 sets of 15 seconds each side

#5 Cat-Camel Stretch

- Starting position: Begin on your hands and knees with weight evenly balanced, stomach muscles activated, back straight.

- Raise your head, then gently arch your back by pressing your stomach towards the floor, your shoulder blades towards each other, and your buttocks towards the ceiling. Hold this stretch for 5 seconds.

- Return to neutral position, and then reverse the stretch by rounding your back towards the ceiling. Look down at floor, tucking your chin towards your chest. Hold this stretch for 5 seconds.
- Keep your stomach muscles activated throughout this movement.
- Relax and return to the starting position.

Repetitions: 10 sets of 5 seconds in each position

#6 *Prayer Stretch*

- Starting position: Begin on your hands and knees with knees directly under the hips and your hands extended out in front of you as in the photo above.

- Next, lean back and push your buttocks against your heels. Hold this stretch for 15 seconds.

- Relax and return to the starting position.

Repetitions: 3 sets of 15 seconds

#7 Learning to Engage Your Core Properly
This is the prerequisite for exercises 8-13.

- Starting position: Lie on your back. Bend your knees and place your feet flat on the floor or mat.
- Place two fingers on your lower abdomen just inside your hips. Put gentle pressure on your fingers towards the floor. This will help you determine if you're doing the exercise properly. To engage your core, you must tighten your abdominal muscles so that you can feel them push against your fingers. This is the telltale sign that you have engaged your core properly. If you do not feel your abdominal muscles pressing against your fingers, then focus on pushing your abdominals outward against your fingers. It will be difficult to keep your abdominal muscles engaged while breathing, but that is the goal. It just takes practice. Once you feel the muscles against your fingers, hold for 10 seconds.

This is the technique to use whenever we use the term, "engage your core."

8 Posterior Pelvic Tilts

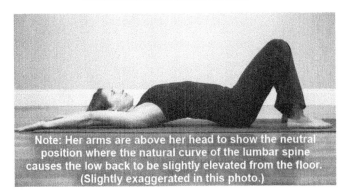

Note: Her arms are above her head to show the neutral position where the natural curve of the lumbar spine causes the low back to be slightly elevated from the floor. (Slightly exaggerated in this photo.)

- Starting position: Lie on your back in a neutral position (see photo). Bend your knees and place your feet flat on the floor or mat. Feet should be shoulder width part. Your arms should be at your side.
- Engage your core.
- Gently tilt your hips towards your face. Your buttocks should not actually leave the floor. You should feel your low back press into the floor or mat. Imagine a bowl of water on your stomach just below your belly button. As you tilt your pelvis, the water would spill towards your face. Hold this position for 10 seconds, while keeping your core engaged.
- Return to starting position

A. Starting Point   B. Ending Point

#9a Half Plank/Plank

- Starting position: Lie on your stomach with your elbows under your shoulders and your forearms resting on the floor or mat, keeping your chest elevated. Your knees should rest on the mat. Bend your knees and lift your feet off the mat.

- Tighten your stomach muscles.
- Lift your body so that only your knees, forearms and elbows remain on the mat.
- Maintain a straight back.
- This may be difficult at first to hold for 30 seconds but that's the goal. Hold for 10 or 20 seconds at first, if that's all you can do. Return to the relaxed position.
- Repeat half plank holding for same amount of time you were able to hold the position.

Repetitions: Build up to 3 sets of 30 seconds each (You may have to start at 3 sets of 10 or 20 seconds each)

#9b Full Plank

Once you are proficient at holding the half plank (previous exercise) for 3 sets of 30 seconds each, substitute for Full Plank, where you lift your body from your toes instead of your knees.

- Starting position: Lie on your stomach with your elbows under your shoulders and your forearms resting on the floor or mat, keeping your chest off the mat. With your legs straight, point your toes into the mat and keep your heels off the mat.

- With your body in a straight line, press through your forearms and toes and lift your body off the mat. Keep your neck aligned with your back and eyes looking towards the floor. Keep your abdominal muscles tight, and hold this position for 30 seconds. Return to the relaxed position.

Repetitions: build up to 3 sets of 30 seconds

#10 Bird Dog

- Starting position: Begin on your hands and knees with your hands directly under your shoulders, and knees directly under your hips, so your weight is evenly balanced. Keep your back straight.

- Raise your left arm forward and tighten your stomach muscles.

- Extend your right leg straight back. **Do Not** lift your leg higher than your hips.
- Keep your back flat and your hips squared. Hold this stretch for 5 seconds.
- Relax and return to the starting position. Repeat on the opposite side.

Repetitions: 10 sets of 5 seconds each position

(See important note regarding your form during this exercise on the next page).

Note: *DO NOT DO THIS:*

This photo shows an incorrect pose. Do NOT rotate the lifted leg, nor raise it higher than your hips.

#11 Crunches/Obliques – Quality NOT Quantity

- Starting position: Lie on your back. Bend your knees and place your feet flat on the floor or mat. Put your hands behind your ears (not your neck). You should try not to use your neck muscles for this exercise.

- Tighten your stomach muscles. Curl up just enough to raise your shoulder blades off the mat. Hold this position for three full seconds.

- Reach your left elbow towards your right hip and hold for three seconds. Return back to the middle neutral position continuing to keep your shoulder blades lifted off the mat. Hold for three seconds in this lifted, neutral position.
- Return to the starting position.
- Repeat on the other side.

  Repetitions: Build up to 3 sets of 10. (Five in each direction).

#12a Side Bridge (Half)

- Starting position: Lie on your left side. Your left forearm is flat on the floor or mat facing front, palm face down on the mat. Your left arm is perpendicular to your body supporting your weight.

- Bend your knees and rest your arm on your top outer leg keeping a straight plane from your head to your knees (as seen above).

- Tighten your abdominal muscles and lift your pelvis in the air. Attempt to maintain a straight line from your right shoulder through your hip down to your right knee. Relax and return to the starting position.
- Hold this elevation for 10 seconds.
- Repeat on the other side.

Repetitions: Build up to 5 sets of a 10 second hold for each side.

12b Side Bridge (Full)

Once you are proficient at holding the Side Bridge (Half) (previous exercise) for 5 sets of 10 seconds each, substitute for Side Bridge (Full).

- Starting position: Lie on your left side. Your left forearm is flat on the floor or mat facing front, palm face down on the mat. Your left arm is perpendicular to your body supporting your weight. Keep your right arm on your outer top leg. You should be in a straight line from shoulder to feet. (Keep your legs straight and on the mat).

- Tighten your abdominal muscles and lift your pelvis in the air. Your entire torso should lift off the mat in a straight line. (Refer to photo above). Attempt to maintain a straight line from your right shoulder through your hip down to your feet. Hold this elevated position for 10 seconds.
- Relax and return to the starting position.
- Repeat on the other side.

Repetitions: Build up to 5 sets of a 10 second hold each time.

#13 Dead Bug

This exercise is only for people who have zero pain and are proficient with the other exercises.

- Starting position: Lie on your back with knees up in the air and bent at a ninety degree angle. Lift your arms straight up towards the ceiling.
- Tighten your abdominal muscles and keep them engaged throughout entire exercise.

- Slowly lower the right arm and left leg so they are parallel to the floor, but just a few inches off the floor. Hold for 5 seconds. Bring arm and leg back to starting position.

- Repeat on the other side: lower the left arm and right leg toward the floor. Hold for 5 seconds.

  Repetitions: Build up to 3 sets of 10 repetitions on each side holding for 5 seconds each time.

Neck Exercises

#1 Chin Retraction

 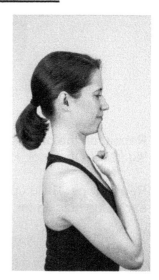

- Sit comfortably in an upright position.
- Place two fingers on your chin. Use your fingers to gently push your head back, along a straight plane. Do not move your chin up or down. Do not tilt your head forward or backward. Now let go of the chin, but stay in this retracted position. Focus specifically on the muscles in the back of your neck. Hold for ten seconds.
- Relax and return to the starting position.

Repetitions: Repeat 10 times holding the retractions for 10 seconds each time

2 Scalene Stretch

- Sit comfortably in an upright position.
- Place your right hand under your right buttock or grasp the chair for stabilization.
- Tilt your head towards your left shoulder.
- Lift your left arm and place your left palm over the top and right side of your head. Your left fingers point toward the floor.
- Using the weight of your left arm to gently stretch your head downward toward your left shoulder. You'll feel the stretch in the right side of your neck. Hold for 15 seconds.
- Relax and return to the starting position.

Repetitions: Repeat 3 times for each side holding each stretch for 15 seconds.

#3 Upper Trapezius Stretch

- Sit comfortably in an upright position.
- Place your right hand under your right buttock or grasp the chair for stabilization.
- Rotate your head 45 degrees to the right (to the side you are anchoring).
- Lift your left arm and place your left palm over the top and right side of your head. Your left fingers point toward the floor.
- Using the weight of your left arm, gently stretch your head downward toward your left hip. You'll feel the stretch in the right side of your neck and the muscle between your neck and your shoulder.
- Hold for 15 seconds.
- Relax and return to the starting position.

Repetitions: Repeat 3 times for each side holding each stretch for 15 seconds.

#4 Levator Scapulae Stretch

- Sit comfortably in an upright position.
- Place your right hand under your right buttock or grasp the chair for stabilization.
- Rotate your head 45 degrees to the left.
- Lift your left arm and place your left palm over the right side of the back of your head.
- Your left fingers point toward the floor.
- Using the weight of your arm stretch your head downward toward your left hip.
- Hold for 15 seconds.
- Relax and return to the starting position.

Repetitions: Repeat 3 times for each side holding each stretch for 15 seconds.

Isometric Exercises for the Neck

Isometric exercises are exercises where we are strengthening a muscle or muscle group without actually moving that muscle or the adjacent joints.

#5a. Neck Isometric Exercise: Flexion

- Sit comfortably in an upright position.
- Place your left or right palm in the middle of your forehead. Your fingers should point upward.
- Your hand should provide gentle, continuous resistance as you try to tilt your head forward as if you're trying to touch your head to your chest. There should be equal pressure from your head going forward and your hand pushing backward so that you're actually not moving in either direction. You'll feel your neck muscles contracting. Apply continuous muscular contraction and continuous resistance for 6 seconds.
- Relax and return to the starting position.

  Repetitions: Repeat 3 times holding each stretch for 6 seconds.

#5b. Neck Isometric Exercise: Extension

- Sit comfortably in an upright position.
- Place your right or left hand on the back of your head.
- Your hand should provide gentle, continuous resistance as you try to tilt your head backward as if you're trying to touch your head to your shoulder blades. There should be equal pressure from your head going backward and your hand pushing foreword so that you're actually not moving in either direction. You'll feel your neck muscles contracting. Apply continuous muscular contraction and continuous resistance for 6 seconds.
- Relax and return to the starting position.

Repetitions: Repeat 3 times for each side holding each stretch for 6 seconds.

#5c Neck Side-Bending Isometric Exercise

- Sit comfortably in an upright position.
- Place your right hand, fingers pointing upward, on the right side of your face directly above your ear.
- Your hand should provide gentle, continuous resistance as you try to tilt your head to the right as if you're putting your right ear toward your right shoulder. There should be equal pressure from your head going right and your hand pushing left so that you're actually not moving in either direction. You'll feel your neck muscles contracting. Apply continuous muscular contraction and continuous resistance for 6 seconds.
- Relax and return to the starting position.
- Repeat on the left side.

Repetitions: Repeat 3 times for each side holding each stretch for 6 seconds.

#5d Neck Rotation – Isometric Exercise

- Sit comfortably in an upright position.
- Place your right hand, fingers pointing upward, on the right side of your face, directly in front of your ear.
- Your hand should provide gentle, continuous resistance as you try to turn your head to the right as if looking over your right shoulder. There should be equal pressure from your head turning right and your hand preventing it so that you're actually not moving in either direction. You'll feel your neck muscles contracting. Apply continuous muscular contraction and continuous resistance for 6 seconds.
- Relax and return to the starting position.
- Repeat on the left side.

Repetitions: Repeat 3 times for each side holding each stretch for 6 seconds.

8

Medical Doctor Testimonials

Dr. Robert Sidlow, M.D., Associate Professor of Medicine at Albert Einstein College of Medicine

As a board-certified internist who has been in practice for  over 13 years, I spend much of my time attempting to alleviate the pain and suffering of my patients. As a clinician, one of the biggest challenges I face is helping my patients deal with musculoskeletal and neuropathic pain syndromes--those all-too-common, yet frequently debilitating--ailments caused by bad backs, pinched nerves, arthritis, and the like. Unfortunately, much of what I have to offer my patients boils down to the following: take a pain pill, stretch if you can, wait, and hope for the best. After a failed trial of "conservative" therapy a call might go out to the orthopedic surgeon for assistance; a truly satisfactory result is not common. The simple fact is that physicians are not well-trained to deal with musculoskeletal pain, and patients can suffer as a result.

Thankfully, my views on this topic have been turned completely upside down since I have personally discovered Dr. Jonathan Donath's outstanding practice. After beginning a vigorous exercise regimen I started to experience awful neck and upper back pain, accompanied by numbness and tingling down my left arm and fingers. For weeks I tried to nurse the pain with non-steroidal anti-inflammatory medication, but the pain persisted and got to the point that I was almost unable to work, sleep, or most importantly, play guitar. I was literally in tears from the excruciating pain. A neurosurgeon diagnosed a herniated disc and pinched nerve in my neck and offered to decompress it with an operation. In desperation I called Dr. Donath instead.

My visit to Dr. Donath's office was an outstanding experience. He spent about an hour with me and combined multiple modalities to fix the herniated disc in my neck: deep massage, active release techniques, traditional manipulation, cold therapy, and finally spinal decompression. After that first hour with Dr. Donath my pain had decreased from a 10/10 down to a manageable 4/10, and I was able to comfortably move my head and neck. That very night I was able to play guitar again. Two days later I went back for another series of treatments and the pain decreased even further. After about five days the pain was absolutely gone. Unbelievable! Since then he has used the same wonderful techniques to help me overcome painful bouts of sciatica as well.

My own patients and family members have become "believers" in Dr. Donath's abilities as well--- the results he achieves are real and lasting. He is my go-to guy for the majority of musculoskeletal and neuropathic pain syndromes that I now realize are truly treatable.

Dr. Gary Kalan, M.D., Head of Anesthesia at Greenwich Hospital, Greenwich, CT

I am a 58 year old anesthesiologist who has suffered from lower back pain for over 20 years. I have tried many therapies in the past including massage, acupuncture, physical therapy, and most recently two epidural steroid injections. An MRI revealed severely degenerative

L5-S1 disc disease and I was recommended to undergo spinal fusion surgery by three neurosurgeons.

I have always been active and exercise regularly, however despite my efforts my pain continued to progress. My pain had advanced to the point of making it difficult to sleep through the night and in the morning it was a strain to bend over to tie my shoes. Getting through a day at work was becoming increasingly difficult. In desperation and with a great degree of skepticism I decided to look into spinal decompression therapy and made an appointment for a consultation with Dr. Jonathan Donath.

I was extremely impressed with his professionalism, thoroughness, and confidence that he would be able to help me with my back problems. I immediately began his intensive program including decompression, nutrition, and slowly incorporated an exercise program. Through these treatments I gradually noticed a significant decrease in my pain and an improving range of motion in my back. I presently sleep through the night pain free, am comfortable at work, and have resumed playing golf without problems. At the present time I have a low level of discomfort and stiffness in my back, but I am more confident than ever that I will eventually be pain free. All of this was done without missing a day of work or undergoing a major surgical procedure.

Dr. Donath has not only made a major improvement in my back pain, but he has become a true friend and colleague. It is my privilege to write this testimonial to his care, and I would strongly urge others suffering from back pain to see Dr. Donath.

Dr. Gregory Galano, M.D., Orthopedic Surgeon in New York and White Plains, NY

As a board-certified sports medicine orthopaedist, I see many patients with activity-related joint, back, and neck pain. Often I am confronted with patients that have exhausted other conservative forms of treatment, but fail to have lasting relief. Many of these patients would like to avoid surgery or may not even be good candidates for surgical procedures.

Dr. Donath has proved extremely helpful to this patient population. He spends a great deal of time listening and examining the patient in order to formulate an individualized treatment plan. He offers innovative treatment options which include chiropractic, active release therapy, Graston technique, non-operative spinal decompression, and even exercise and nutrition programs.

Having shared many patients with Dr. Donath, I have seen firsthand the positive interventions he has made in their daily lives and activities. They express the utmost respect and confidence in his clinical evaluation and knowledge, as well as his treatment techniques. I have no reservations recommending him highly to any patient I think may benefit from his services.

Dr. Dawn Garcen, M.D., Family Medicine/Urgent Care, White Plains, NY

 I had been experiencing lower back pain for at least 6-7 months before I had visited Dr. Donath's office. Prior to this, I had tried doing stretches at home, taking some medications and getting acupuncture, but despite this, things did not improve. In fact, my symptoms only progressed and became unbearable. It was so difficult to get out of bed in the morning, work my 12 hour shifts as a physician in Urgent Care and do my daily work outs, which I enjoyed so much. My colleague at work, who is also a physician and patient of Dr. Donath, recommended I see him and I was so glad I did.

On my first visit, he patiently listened to my story and examined me carefully. He took his time to discuss possible diagnoses, sent me for an MRI that day, and saw me the next day to discuss results, and potential treatment plan. I listened to his advice and began spinal decompression, which was the best decision I have ever made. After a few visits, my pain started to subside and shortly I became pain-free. I currently still am in treatment and doing exercises as per Dr. Donath's advice, but I am so much better thanks to his care.

Dr. Donath and his staff are knowledgeable and very professional. I am so grateful to them for getting me back to my normal life. I highly recommend him to anyone who is having back pain.

Dr. Chris Whitney, D.O., Sackler Center for Pain Management at Greenwich Hospital, Greenwich, CT

As a board-certified pain management physician, I understand the importance of delivering multi-disciplinary care for my patients. I also understand, however, the difficulty patients often encounter in finding the "right" provider for their condition. Fortunately, I have had the pleasure of working with Dr. Jonathan Donath and have seen firsthand the outstanding results of his treatments. Dr. Donath's professionalism, expertise, and caring bed side manner immediately put patients at ease. The feedback that I receive from my patients who Dr. Donath has cared for is consistently positive. I was so impressed with his results and the feedback I received from my patients that I personally visited Dr. Donath's office in an attempt to experience what my patients were reporting to me. Upon meeting Dr. Donath and his staff, I immediately understood why my patients are so impressed, not only with his treatments but with him as an individual. Having a history of low back pain myself, I was eager to try some of his treatments. In particular, I found the decompression to be a comfortable and relaxing experience. As with my patients who are seeking a non-invasive treatment for pain, I encourage anyone suffering with pain to arrange a consultation with Dr. Donath as he is the "top of his field" and a truly compassionate chiropractor who delivers the right care for the right patient. It is my pleasure to write this testimonial on behalf of Dr. Donath.

Dr. Annebeth Litt, M.D., White Plains, NY

Dr. Donath is amazing. As an internist, I have to decide

between traditional western medicine and chiropractic care for my patients with back pain and other joint-related complaints. Dr. Donath's thorough and comprehensive approach to care allows my patients to get relief faster and less invasively. The result is invariably positive. One of my patients said he got his life and golf game back after seeing Dr. Donath. Another said that he (Dr. Donath) was able to get rid of a pain she had for over 5 years in just a few sessions. I can confirm his success first-hand: Dr. Donath relieved my chronic pain with multiple techniques: manipulation, spinal decompression, vitamins and supplements, exercise and stretching. His hands-on approach and love of his work is reflected by the excellent results he gets. I continue to send my friends, family, and patients to Dr. Donath because I know he gets results.

Dr. Eugene Dinkevich, M.D., Mount Vernon, NY

I am a pediatrician and in my work I have to bend down a lot and I'm constantly lifting kids. I usually have one to three bad flare ups of low back pain every year. When my back would "go out", I could barely walk to the bathroom and would have to lie down in bed for a few days. I have tried everything: doing nothing and "toughing it out", muscle relaxants, physical therapy, chiropractic, therapeutic massage, and even painful steroid injections. Nothing worked.

When I moved to Westchester, I met Dr. Jonathan Donath. In just a couple of sessions with Dr. Donath, the pain completely disappeared. If it hadn't happened to me, I wouldn't have believed it. During my last flare up, I was expecting to be on my back for 2-3 days and in pain for 2 weeks. Instead, after one session with Dr. Donath, I was able to walk; two more sessions and I was fine. I could walk, bend down and I had almost no pain. Since that last back episode, Dr. Donath has helped me with my tendonitis in my right hand and with my chronic knee problems. I recommend Dr. Donath to everyone with back, muscle or joint pain. Even if you have not had relief with other treatments and other Chiropractors, give Dr. Donath a chance. I did and he changed my life.

Dr. Steven Kubersky, M.D., Internal Medicine Yonkers, NY

Over the last several years, I have referred dozens of

 patients to Dr. Donath. My patients have uniformly returned pleased. They have been impressed with his thoroughness and professionalism. Most importantly, they experience relief from their symptoms! Dr. Donath has become my "go-to" chiropractor of choice.

Dr. Sean Misciagna, M.D., Family Medicine/Urgent Care, White Plains, NY

After dealing with aching, burning neck and back pain

related to daily use of computers, tablets, etc., my colleague, also an Urgent Care physician, suggested I see Dr. Donath. It was the best advice I could have taken. After a thorough medical history and physical exam, Dr. Donath arrived at a diagnosis, explained how it occurred and how it causes pain, and then explained a course of treatment and why it would relieve pain. All the while, Dr. Donath was talking with me so that we could get to know each other; he also offered simple advice to contribute to pain relief.

To my delight, but not surprise, after 8 visits over 3 weeks, my pain had resolved. I'm using the advice Dr. Donath gave me at my first consultation and every visit thereafter to help prevent the pain from returning. Furthermore, I offer the same advice to my patients and refer them to Dr. Donath when they report symptoms similar to mine.

Dr. Carol A. Grant, M.D., Gastroenterologist Bronx, New York

I am someone who was very skeptical about chiropractors but when my mother developed severe neck and back pain I knew that she needed help beyond what her medical doctors could do. My husband, who is also a physician, suggested that she contact Dr. Donath who had helped him with his lower back pain before and was very pleased with the care and attention that he had received.

My mother consulted him and after two weeks she was pain free and able to resume her regular activities. Since that time, Dr. Donath has treated many members of my family and friends. He is prompt, professional and kind. Most importantly, his treatments make people better.

Dr. Harold Weissman, M.D., Ophthalmic Surgeon, Lenox Hill Hospital, New York, NY

My wife actually went to Dr. Donath before I did. She was

experiencing terrible neck pain and literally could not move her neck in any direction without excruciating pain. It was so bad that initially she was unable to drive herself to Dr. Donath's office. After only two spinal decompression treatments by Dr. Donath, she was able to resume driving. Following a few weeks of treatment, she was pain free and her range of motion was back to normal.

A few years later, I started having arm and elbow pain. I tweaked something in my arm while working out and anti-inflammatory medication and pain killers did not help. The problem affected my ability to function as an eye surgeon. I saw Dr. Donath who diagnosed my condition as lateral epicondylitis (more commonly known as tennis elbow). He treated me utilizing Active Release Techniques and I improved almost immediately. He also gave me numerous exercises to do at home. After three visits to his office, my pain was completely gone. I highly recommend Dr. Donath to my family, friends, and patients who experience any sort of musculoskeletal pain.

Dr. Daniel Gold, M.D., Head and Neck Surgeon at ENT and Allergy Associates, White Plains, NY

Dr. Donath is an excellent clinician. His understanding of  the root cause of disease allows him to accurately target the symptoms, and relieve suffering. His techniques of pain relief succeed where many traditional medical therapies may have failed. His bedside manner engenders trust and a feeling of partnership with his patients. His therapies well complement and extend what is possible to accomplish with more traditional medicine. He is a valued member of the larger medical community, and the Westchester community is fortunate to have him in our area.

Dr. Amy Silverman, M.D., Millwood, NY

I am so grateful to Dr. Donath and his staff for the wonderful care I received these past few months. I experienced a recurrence of a herniated disc in my back and could hardly walk or move. The thought of how much physical therapy I went through before I felt better the last time, and how quickly the pain recurred, made me very pessimistic. A friend had recommended spinal decompression therapy with Dr. Donath and originally I was quite skeptical. But, I thought it was worth a try. I did the treatments for a few months and my pain lessened so much that there are times I forget I ever *had* pain! I am now able to exercise again as well as to do everything that I want to do. I also like the warm atmosphere in the office. I would highly recommend Dr. Donath and this treatment.

Dr. Daniel Tare, M.D., Urologist sub-specializing in minimally invasive procedures and robotic surgery, Mount Kisco, NY

A few months ago, I hurt my neck. I don't even know what I had done but several days had passed and my range of motion was still severely restricted and I was getting tired of the pain. A close colleague of mine urged me to go see Dr. Donath. I had honestly never even considered going to a chiropractor but pain can be a strong motivating factor. Dr. Donath impressed me with his knowledge and diagnostic skills. He said I had strained a joint in my neck and the muscles surrounding the joint were in spasm to protect the injury. He treated both my neck muscles and joints. I was sore immediately after treatment but my range of motion had improved significantly. By the next morning I had zero pain and haven't had any since. I have subsequently sent some of my own patients to Dr. Donath for low back pain and received excellent feedback. I highly recommend him.

Dr. Jay Weinberger, M.D., Board Certified Anesthesiologist at Phelps Memorial Hospital, Sleepy Hollow, NY

 I am an active 52 year old physician, whose back 'goes out' every few years. I had minimally invasive back surgery two years ago to address this issue. I was well for a while after the surgery and then the pain returned. It was on a less severe level, but became almost constant. I was treated by Dr. Donath, and in a matter of a few weeks was essentially pain free. I have also been successfully treated by Dr. Donath for tennis elbow, which he essentially healed in a matter of weeks. While not all pains and physical problems can be treated through chiropractic, I believe Dr. Donath is sincere and candid in his assessment, and if he is confident he can help, so am I.

129

Dr. Jason Moshe Shuker, M.D., Family Medicine/Urgent Care White Plains, NY

The most important thing in my life is my family – my wife

and two boys. Most of what I do and don't do is for and because of them.

When I started having neck pain it didn't bother me too much, even after days turned to weeks and then months. But when I started approaching a year of pain, I finally decided to do something about it. I was worried about how it might affect my ability to play with my kids.

I went to see an orthopedist who is a great physician and got great help from him. We went through x-rays and MRIs and came up with a treatment plan. Unfortunately, I was getting worse until I finally had weird sensations in the tips of my fingers. We talked about possibly doing injections into my neck to help with the pain. That made me a little nervous. I have great faith in my physicians, but was apprehensive about needles being stuck into my neck. My wife, who is also a physician, suggested I go see Dr. Donath who had helped her with her migraines and low back pain. I went to see Dr. Donath who offered me an alternative: non-surgical spinal decompression therapy. He said it would take a commitment from me to the therapy, but he was always supportive and optimistic about where I was and where I could be. He and his staff were warm and welcoming at every visit. The treatments were relaxing and painless. The setting actually allowed me to have time to relax my mind as well and clear my thoughts while I was there.

Lo and behold, the finger sensations stopped, and the pain improved. Even months after stopping treatment, I have some 'bad days' – especially after a day running around with the boys - but I am far better than I was before the treatment with Dr. Donath. I am so grateful for how much he helped. Patients of mine continue to see him because he's knowledgeable, he listens well, and most importantly he gets results.

Dr. Susan S. Blum, M.D., M.P.H., Assistant Clinical Professor Department of Preventive Medicine, The Mount Sinai School of Medicine in New York City, Founder and Director Blum Center For Health

I have had the pleasure of working with Dr. Donath during the 5 years that we worked under the same roof at Full Circle Family Care. Not only did we work together, but thankfully, he treated and fixed my shoulder issues.
I recommend him highly, and still send my patients to him, even though I am now at Blum Center for Health.

Dr. Pankaj Jain, M.D., New York, NY

I really don't have words to express my feelings about the care I got in the last 3 months. I was almost handicapped, living with terrible pain all the time, crippling my day to day life. I am a medical doctor and work in a hospital with all sorts of amazing physicians, but after seeing a physical therapist, getting epidural steroids injections, many orthopedists and neurosurgeons, finally my destination lead me to see Dr. Jonathan Donath. With great skepticism, I laid down for spinal decompression therapy. It was unbelievable that after only two initial sessions, my radiating pain down my leg had almost disappeared. Gradually, I started getting better, started doing exercises that they gave me midway through the treatment. Now, I am doing all my daily activities without any pain.

I highly recommend Dr. Jonathan for any problems related to the musculoskeletal system; you will definitely feel at home and will get better.

Dr. Steven Farkas, M.D., Radiologist, Mount Kisco Medical Group

I hurt my shoulder playing basketball and nothing seemed  to help. A colleague of mine encouraged me to go see Dr. Donath. I was incredibly skeptical that a chiropractor would be able to improve my pain and range of motion when nothing else had helped. I desperately wanted to avoid surgery so I was willing to try anything. He treated me one time and I couldn't believe how much better I felt the next day. Within a week I was pain free. I've also seen the remarkable improvement of some of his patients' herniated discs on MRI. I would strongly recommend anyone with musculoskeletal pain or disc issues to see Dr. Donath before considering surgery.

Dr. Hedi L. Leistner, M.D., Pediatric Pulmonologist at NYU Langone Medical Center

Dr. Jonathan Donath helped me in 2012 after I fell on

some ice. The MRI revealed a tear in my left supraspinatus tendon superimposed on moderate to severe tendinosis of the rotator cuff muscles. Dr. Donath's therapy decreased my pain so that I could then participate successfully in physical therapy. I am certain that I was able to avoid surgery because of Dr. Donath's efforts.

Dr. Mamadou Souare, M.D., New York, NY

In my 8 years as a general surgeon in Africa, I have been

thanked by many patients. I never really understood how valuable getting someone out of pain was until I became a patient myself. I had been experiencing terrible back pain and nothing helped. After treatment from Dr. Donath, I couldn't believe how much better I felt.

Above all, I was so impressed by the way that Dr. Donath took care of me and walked me through everything he was doing. I learned more from him in one hour than I had in a month of certain classes in medical school. Thank you Dr. Donath. I will definitely see you again.

Dr. Jenifer Johnson, M.D., Family Medicine/Urgent Care, White Plains, NY

As a board certified family physician, I am very open to the  idea of "complementary" medical therapies which may be beneficial to my patients, as an adjunct or alternative to traditional medicine. The challenge, I find, is developing relationships with providers in the area that I feel comfortable referring patients to when I am confident they might benefit from this care. Luckily, my own search for chiropractic care led me to Dr. Jonathan Donath. Not only has he been able to help me with a variety of issues, from migraine headaches to pregnancy related back pain to exercise related ailments, but he has proven to be a valuable resource to me as an urgent care physician.

Doctors usually make the worst patients, and I am no exception. I usually call on Dr. Donath in some moment of desperation, when some ailment or injury is preventing me from keeping up with my busy life. In "short order" (usually one or two visits, because I rarely have more time than that!) he is able to get me some relief and break the cycle of discomfort, as well as provide me with tips or exercises to remedy the root of the problem. Some of the patients I refer to Dr. Donath are in need of this kind of specific targeted treatment for a painful condition--I know that based on my own experience, Dr. Donath will be able to give them some relief in one or two treatments which might ameliorate their need for other medications, as well as provide them with exercises and modification of activities to prevent the pain in the future. The other category of patient he has been able help are those who have a more chronic condition--those who have "tried everything" that conventional medicine can offer them, and still have pain or disability. I am happy to be able to provide those patients an option that they might not have explored yet. Additionally, it is nice to be able to assure these patients that I have personal experience with Dr. Donath and that he has helped me--he is not just another name on a piece of paper.

Dr. David Stemerman, M.D., Radiologist and Owner of Open High Field MRI and CT of Westchester, Larchmont, NY

While I have not been a patient of Dr. Donath, as a

Radiologist, I deal with Dr. Donath frequently going over cases and dealing with issues that arise concerning patients. Dr. Donath is caring, concerned, and always seems to have the patient's interest on top of his list, making sure they are taken care of properly. He is interested in learning about the abnormalities I find, and he doesn't just read the reports of the studies he receives, but looks at the images and correlates them with the patient's symptoms to try to make their therapy better. He is a very caring individual.

Though I was not a patient of Dr. Donath's, I do have personal experience with someone close to me who was a patient. The person was in intense pain due to a disc herniation. The patient had been to several surgeons and pain management specialists and was given a choice of either surgery or suffer. Pain management treatments as well did not seem to alleviate the discomfort. The patient is an athlete and did not want to undergo surgery for many reasons but could not bear the pain anymore. Finally, the patient found Dr. Donath, and through his therapy, found relief. Now the patient is off of all pain medications, is functioning as an athlete again, and avoided all of the issues surrounding back surgery. The patient found Dr. Donath's approach healing when other therapies were not.

Dr. Sumith Roy M.D., Valley Cottage, NY

I would like to thank Dr. Donath for his advice and the

treatment I received for back pain. I am currently in my 5th month of pregnancy and am doing pretty well. I had sciatica of my right leg and suffered unbearable pain with numbness restricting my daily activities. I must say, after receiving treatment from Dr. Donath, I did not have to take any pain medications and with 3 treatments, I was doing incredibly well. I have never received any prior chiropractic treatment and hence was quite apprehensive at first but am very glad that I came to the right place and thankfully am now pain free!!!

Thank you Dr. Donath. My husband and I truly appreciate your help!!

Dr. Alain A. Le Guillou, M.D., FAAP, Larchmont, NY

Dr. Donath has demonstrated a wide range of skills in the

treatment of various musculoskeletal conditions, going beyond a traditional chiropractic approach to improve accident prevention, or postural and structural conditions. My patients and I have all appreciated his warm and congenial approach and how quickly his methods allowed a full return to activities and play!

Dr. Barry Feuer, M.D., Internal Medicine

There is only one chiropractor I trust with my patients and that is Dr. Jonathan Donath. He is extremely effective in reducing and alleviating most types of musculoskeletal pain. I recommend him highly.

Dr. Rittu Kapoor, M.D., Pediatric Anesthesiologist at Phelps Memorial Hospital, Sleepy Hollow, NY

I went from being an over energetic and over enthusiastic doctor to a person in Pain! Pain! Pain! I had pain in my elbow, arm, and forearm, and it was slowly restricting my shoulder and neck too. Woke up in pain which only got worse with daily routine. This went on for about 4 months which is when my colleague told me about Dr. Donath.

In spite of being Skeptical... I went to him as he came highly recommended. And I had already tried an orthopedic doctor and physical therapy.

This was a turning point in my life!!!!

At my first visit, he should have really been with his son, who had been diagnosed with a fracture and was put in a cast the very same afternoon, but instead of canceling my appointment, he stood there patiently listening to my saga. He spent over 2 hours listening and coming up with a game plan and answering all my questions. I felt very positive and reassured. He started treatment the very first time and even called me at home that night to check on my pain scale and answer any other questions I had. During the course of treatment, he was always very pleasant, thoughtful, and thorough. He even helped me with my knee and sacroiliac joint pain as well. He took care of more than two extra pain complaints in the same appointment which made him spend almost triple the time each session.

I am thankful to Dr. Donath and will highly recommend him for treatment of elbow, shoulder, knee, and back issues. I am pain free now and have resumed my daily activities with full force and more.

Dr. Nancy Manzione, M.D., Gastroenterologist at Montefiore Medical Center, Bronx, NY

I'm a busy gastroenterologist in the Bronx doing numerous endoscopic procedures each week. I love my job and have been doing it for over 30 years. I also thrive on moderate exercise…rowing, bicycling, swimming, walking, and my "shake weight." I have a high tolerance for pain, but no tolerance for incapacitation!! Call me Type A. So, when I suddenly herniated a C6-C7 disc, I needed a fix and I needed it fast. "Uncle!" This pain was indeed intolerable!! Maximum doses of nonsteroidals and Neurontin didn't make a dent, and Percocet appeared to be a placebo…didn't even give me a high!! A colleague's husband recommended Dr. Donath and his Non-Surgical Spinal Decompression Therapy.

Although Dr. Donath warned me it could take a couple of months to get back to baseline, within a few sessions I was able to work at reduced volume and now after 2 months I'm off all meds and back to meeting all the demands of my busy practice. Now that the snow is gone, I'm back on my bicycle, will soon take my gym membership off suspension, and can't wait to swim in our condo's newly renovated pool. Though difficult for a Type A, I did promise Dr. Donath I'd take it slow. I hope that testimonials from patients will eventually convince insurance companies to cover such valuable treatment.

One more thing: the machine works, but the TLC from Dr. Donath and his staff, including the flexibility for scheduling treatments, added to the speedy recovery. I'm so grateful to them for helping me get my life back.

With serious gratitude.

9

Patient Testimonials

Dr. Donath has received hundreds of written as well as video testimonials from patients. Many of them can be seen at www.backpainwestchester.com.

Here are just a few examples:

Dr. Alyce S. - Scarsdale, NY

In October of 2011, the mild lower back pain I had experienced for some time with every change in the weather became severe and debilitating. I could no longer stand up straight without severe pain. I could not sleep because every turn in bed caused enough pain to wake me up. Dr. Donath had me undergo an MRI. The diagnosis: two bulging disks and one herniated disk with some spinal stenosis.

He immediately set up a treatment plan, prescribing spinal decompression 3 times per week, decreasing to twice a week then to once a week. Over 3 months I felt increasing relief and recovered my ability to sleep without interruption and for the first time in over 25 years, I was pain-free.

Dr. Donath gave me a series of exercises to strengthen the muscles supporting my lower back and core to ensure that I was more resistant to injury and remain pain free.

It's difficult to describe how grateful I am for Dr. Donath's detailed treatment and rehabilitation regimen and for his careful monitoring of every stage of my treatment. He has returned me to an active life. I can lift my grandchildren and play with them without fear of pain. Kudos also to his staff, what an amazing group. Thank you all!

Robert D. - Pelham Manor, NY

I started having horrific pain in my butt for several days. The pain reached an unbearable level when it started to travel down to my shin. The pain got so bad that I truly wanted to die. I would wake up in the middle of the night in agony. I couldn't stand on my feet for any length of time because of the pain. My wife had to feed me my meals upstairs. I never came down. If I did, I would sit on a chair and moan in pain.

My wife remembered that Dr. Donath had once helped me before for some jaw pain. She went on his website and read that he uses Non-Surgical Spinal Decompression Therapy for back problems. So off we went to see Dr. Donath, me in pain so bad that I was limping. He examined me and sent me for an MRI. It turned out that I had a bulging disc and a severe herniated disc in my low back. My first question was, "Can you help me?" He said, "Yes, I can". I was so relieved to hear him say that. He explained how the machine works to retract the disc back into place and he put me on the machine that very day for my first treatment. The next day my pain was literally all gone. He told me the pain would probably return and while I have had a twinge here and there it never returned like before. Now, several weeks later, my wife has to remind me to take it easy because I'm pain free.

Let me tell you that Dr. Donath is a miracle worker. Without him and his machine, I would still be in agony and only getting worst with no relief in sight. Dr. Donath even called my home on the first night to make sure that I was okay after the first treatment. He treats his patients on a first name basis and is very concerned about your welfare. Dr. Donath and his staff are the best. His associate

Dr. Rambarat even remembers which music I prefer listening to. She is so comforting and knowledgeable and pleasant to speak with. His receptionist is also very efficient. She greets you with a cheerful smile and is always ready to take my ice pack to place it in the freezer while I'm getting treatment.

If you have back pain I would recommend that you see Dr. Donath before you consider seeing a back surgeon. You will not be sorry. He will help you get better without surgery. I know this because he helped me. You will be thanking Dr. Donath as I am.

 **Melissa D. -Somers, NY**

I am a 48 year old woman who injured my neck and back in February of 2010. I sustained 2 cervical disc herniations as well as an injury to the upper thoracic area of my spine. After much blood work, x-rays, an MRI and endless sleepless nights, the many doctors I sought out for relief recommended physical therapy, pain medication, and cervical traction. While these treatments provided some relief, the pain, stiffness, and chronic soreness never completely went away.

In addition, I experienced two setbacks where I threw my back out at work and found myself back at ground zero in terms of healing and pain management. I became desperate that I would have to live out the rest of my life in chronic pain and be dependent on pain medication! After 16 months of frustration and being told that the next steps were shots and surgery, I decided to try spinal decompression with Dr. Donath and the rest is history! After several treatments I became pain free and was able to wean myself off of the muscle relaxants and pain medications for the first time in over a year and a half! I feel as if I have my life back and will be eternally grateful to Dr. Donath, his staff and this new technology for what has been, in my opinion, a miracle!! I recommend this painless, relaxing treatment to anyone who suffers with neck or back pain!! :)

Carlysle M. -Ossining, NY

For many years I have had lower back pain. Five years ago an MRI revealed spinal stenosis, a bulging disc and degenerative disc disease. I have done chiropractic, physiotherapy, and acupuncture, all of which helped in varying degrees but the pain persisted to the point where I couldn't stand for any length of time without feeling intense pain.

I was referred to a neurosurgeon but after the consultation decided that neither surgery nor epidural injections would be an option. Research on the internet led me to Dr. Jonathan Donath and Non-Surgical Spinal Decompression. I met with Dr. Donath for what was an informative and extensive evaluation and decided on the therapy.

After a few weeks of treatment, I have been pain free. What stands out in my mind is the warmth of the reception from Dr. Donath and his entire staff; their care and concern was exceptional. The treatment was pain free and relaxing. My experience was a good one and I now recommend Dr. Donath unreservedly to anyone I know with chronic back pain.

Barbara E. M. -Jamaica W.I.

I give thanks to the Almighty God for answering my prayers. It is he who made my cousin in NY find the article explaining about the Non-Surgical Spinal Decompression Treatment and paved the way for me to come from Jamaica to spend the past 3 months in NY to be treated by Dr. Donath and his caring team.

Five years ago (February 2007), I experienced a fall from a chair which resulted in terrible lower back pains. I tried to get healing in the following ways: Three sets of x-rays done to identify the injury, visits to the orthopedic surgeon, visits to the pain specialist, sessions on the special bed to align my back, twenty (20) sessions of physiotherapy in 2011, ingesting dozens of prescribed and over the counter pain tablets (various types), use of various pain ointments, & use of heating pads. At best, I got some temporary relief. In October 2011, the condition began to deteriorate. In January 2012, I had to employ the use of a cane while having difficulty to climb stairs, kneel and get up from kneeling. In February to March 2012, the pains became worse as the pain tablets, ointments and heating pads were of little effect. I experienced sleepless nights, excruciating pains that literally made me wail in agony, and extreme difficulty in moving between the bedroom and the bathroom. My whole life was now altered.

I was not willing to get the surgery done on my back. My family members prayed to God Almighty to provide deliverance to help me in my distress. It was during this time that my cousin read an article on the spinal decompression treatment and told me about Dr. Donath. The MRI he sent me for showed that I was severely injured with herniated discs in my lumbar region. He and his team of Dr. Kavita, April, and Midori displayed such care, concern, patience and love. From the very beginning I was addressed by my first name and didn't feel like a number like I had gotten used to feeling at other doctors' offices. A warm smile and greeting welcomed me each visit to the clinic.

Dr. Donath is a gift from God with a passion to care for others. He treats you as an individual. He knows exactly where to locate stubborn pains and how to deal with them with his powerful pair of hands and amazing machines. His positive attitude strengthens your faith to get well.

The pains in my back are now gone and those in my right leg have minimized to a scale of 2 out of 10 and getting better. I have again started to sleep and dream. I can again kneel to pray and my singing, smiles and laughter are back. I am happy.

May God continue to bless Dr. Donath and his lovely team of caregivers. I love you all.

Elizabeth P. -Hawthorne, NY

I lost my job and have been on disability since 2005 due to Herniated Disks, Degenerative Disk Disease, Arthritis, Spinal Stenosis and various other ailments in my neck and spine. Compounding this, I have Fibromyalgia and am in severe pain 24/7. After several visits to my very prestigious, prominent neurosurgeon, his prognosis was; "inoperable." He said that during surgery, my disks could potentially crumble. He also said that I would need a brace to support my neck and head. When I told this doctor that I was thinking about trying "Spinal Decompression Therapy."

he strongly recommended that I did not have it done, nor would he be responsible for the consequences. At that point, I could barely hold my neck up. In desperation and pain, I sought out Dr. Jonathan Donath.
I arrived for our first meeting armed with my MRI's and in a lot of pain. I was skeptical of the "Free" consultation! Dr. Donath immediately put me at ease. He was very serious and "passionate" about treating and relieving my pain. He was confident that it at least could be reduced. He went thru my MRI reports with me, explaining them in lay terms. Dr. Donath exuded confidence and gave me the faith to believe that it just may work. And, the consultation really was free!

As of this writing, I have finished my treatments to my upper neck, C-4, C-5 and C-6. My compliance was bittersweet. I did some things that I know I shouldn't have that set me back. I still have limited range and mobility of my neck. But what I don't have is the searing pain that use to accompany every movement of my head. Below are the positive results of my Spinal Decompression Therapy:
1). While driving, I am now able to turn my head from side to side when I come to a stop sign, instead of moving my whole body.
2). I am now able to sit at the computer for an hour or two. "Compliance" would be an hour!
3). I no longer have to wear a neck brace. I am now able to do the prescribed isometric exercises, and have returned to my toning and home-made yoga routine without getting "locked up" on one side.
4). I have days when I have absolutely no pain in that part of the neck, as long as I behave, and use the ice packs!
5). The tingling in my arms and shoulders have all but dissipated.
6). I can now lift my neck with minimal support and less pain.

7). I can carry light items and lift up to 3 pounds.
8). I can now walk again; only 1/2 mile at a time, but that's better than not walking at all.

Dr. Donath has given me back mobility that I thought I would never have again! Given the proper treatment, and the right doctor; especially a doctor who believes better than you do, that all things are possible with the right attitude and faith; then hope can spring to life once more. The treatments themselves were relaxing. Dr. Donath put on cool music for me to listen to, dimmed the lights and told me to relax. And I really did. I will sing Dr. Donath's praises! In plain English, he is such a doll. He's a down to earth guy and a pleasure to have as a caretaker. He has a highly unusual, calming bed-side manner. He offers much advice and knowledge and listens to what you have to say and regards it personally, giving positive feedback and encouragement. He goes above and beyond the call of duty. He gets involved in your total care, understanding other underlying medical issues.

Dr. Donath believed when I was skeptical. He was optimistic when I was pessimistic. He told me I could win when I felt defeated. He truly put his heart and soul into my healing. I know he had more confidence in the outcome than I did! I try not to screw up, but when I do, 15 minutes on ice, and I'm good!

Dr. Donath knew that only part of me was going to heal and that my compounded problems will need work also, but I think that he too is quite happy with the successful outcome. I'm forever grateful for the totality of his care and his passion for healing. God Bless "Dr. D."

George T. -Mount Vernon, NY

Towards the end of August 2010, I was involved in a freak accident. I fell out of a golf cart and was left with a large bruise on my leg and various cuts and scratches. As it turned out, these injuries were the least of my problems. In the coming weeks, I woke up each morning with severe pain running down the outside of my left leg. The pain was constant and ultimately made its way down to my calf and then my ankle.
I was willing to try anything to make it stop. After a friend recommended that I try acupuncture, I read some online reviews and then headed to Manhattan to give it a try. I found that acupuncture gave only fleeting relief, and it did not even temporarily address the piercing sensation I felt each morning. After trying several other options (including cupping, pain medications and even infomercial items), I googled all sorts of remedies. Finally, I typed in "Non-Surgical Back Care for Sciatica, Westchester," and this led me to Dr. Donath. Little did I know that Google was about to help me put my life back together.

I first visited Dr. Donath at the end of September. He ordered an MRI, which revealed that I had 2 herniated discs and 1 bulging disc. Dr. Donath told me that I was a good candidate for his spinal decompression machine. He encouraged me by saying that he expected that this treatment, coupled with an exercise routine that he put together for me, would have me completely healthy and back exercising and playing sports within a few months. I began the treatment that day and it turned out to be one of the best decisions of my life. My sciatica began to disappear within a week and, finally, I was able to get in and out of my car without a burning pain. Just prior to Thanksgiving, I was back at the gym (doing exercises recommended by Dr. Donath) and by Christmas, I was pain free. My biggest accomplishment occurred on February 1, 2011. As a member of the Multiple Myeloma Team, I ran up the stairs to the top of the Empire State Building. In sum, four months after meeting Dr. Donath, I ran up 86 flights of stairs. The following month, I attended a 3 day golf clinic that involved taking roughly 1000 swings and still, I am pain-free. Not only did Dr. Donath fix me in a relatively short time frame, he is a great guy and has a wonderful staff. I am indebted to him and highly recommend him and his caring staff. They saved my back and my sanity.

Susan G. -Riverdale, NY

Before my encounter with Dr. Donath, I had been living in pain for over 7 years. My problem was a herniated disk in my neck. In addition to sometimes unbearable neck pain, I experienced headaches, dizziness and a limited range of motion in my right arm and hand. I make my living as a makeup artist and not having a full range of motion had a negative impact on my ability to do my job. Some days it was nearly impossible to hold a pen and write my name. I had gone to an osteopath, an acupuncturist and two different chiropractors. After many years of treatment (and many, many thousands of dollars) my range of motion was only slightly better. Any improvement made in the level of pain I experienced was minimal and temporary at best.

Several years ago while on vacation, my husband and I were introduced to spinal decompression through an advertisement we saw on a local television station. My husband has suffered with lower back pain for most of his adult life and was intrigued by the procedure we saw being demonstrated. When we got home, he immediately started searching for a doctor in our area. After researching local specialists, we decided to call Dr. Donath based on the many incredible testimonials we saw. For me, a combination of spinal decompression, manual adjustments and ART has been a game changer. I have regained my quality of life and have a more positive outlook on just about everything! I maintain my progress with monthly visits and Dr. Donath and his staff are always a pleasure to deal with.

Charlie M. -Long Island, NY

As a long time back pain sufferer (31 years), I finally found a treatment that really works. I have lived with pain and discomfort for most of my life. There were times when I literally could not stand up and was bed ridden for days. Herniated disk, pinched nerves, degenerated disk, torn muscle I had them all. Nothing seemed to help solve the problem. I was convinced that the solution was surgery. Then one night I was flipping through the channels and came across an infomercial for spinal decompression. I went on their web site the next day and was linked to Dr. Jonathan Donath. He offered to have me come in and give his active release techniques and spinal decompression treatment methods a try.

Where was this treatment 30 years ago? After only five to six visits I felt like a completely different person. In the past I could not stand up or sit down for long periods of time without pain. I just came back from Disney World. I spent 7 days walking and standing on long lines with my 4 and 5 year old. I came back with virtually no pain at all. To me this is my Magical world, to be pain free. Trust me, if you are considering surgery STOP and check this out first. It is definitely worth a shot. Thank you Dr. Donath.

Guarionex P. -Bronx, NY

I have been suffering from shoulder and neck pain for over 15 years now. It started while I was serving in the United States Marines. I was treated in Japan, Yale medical school, and most recently in New York. I have seen many doctors for this and have tried all sources of exercise programs. It used to get better for a couple of months and then the pain and discomfort would return and my life was miserable again. One day, I was looking in the internet and saw this spinal decompression method by Dr. Donath, and desired to give it a try. That has been the best thing that ever happened to me. It really works! The pain on my neck was the first thing to go, then the shoulder, and finally the pain on the back of my right arm. I played golf yesterday, and I felt great. I want to thank you doctor. I have not felt this good in a very long time.

Blanca P. -White Plains, NY

In July 2011, while exercising, I injured my lower back. I have suffered from lower back pain for a few years, but always recuperated after a few days. This pain that I was feeling was different. I was in excruciating pain all day long. I was taking muscle relaxants and strong pain medication. The medication worked for a short period of time but made me so drowsy that I could not perform simple daily activities. One day, I was lying down because of severe pain, at some point I tried to move positions and was not able to do so. I felt paralyzed, scared and started to panic. I thought I was never going to be able to get out of bed or go back to work.

My friend had seen Dr. Donath's ad and recommended that I go and see him. I gave her all the excuses to not go, I became desperate and decided to make an appointment. When I arrived to his office, I was in no mood to smile at anyone who smiled at me. I thought no one could know what I was going through. Dr. Donath showed concern and started asking me questions about my condition. He knew at that point what was wrong with my back, but he needed me to have an MRI to confirm his diagnosis. I was so surprised at the way Dr. Donath explained in such detail how the spine worked and the reason behind herniated discs. After he received the results of the MRI, he again discussed in detail a plan of action. I value the time and concern that Dr. Donath put in to giving me hope that I was going to feel better soon. He explained how the spinal decompression therapy worked, how many sessions it would take and the financial plans available.

The first time that I went for therapy, I was scared, and he assured me that I was not going to feel any pain. He was correct I didn't feel any pain. During the next few sessions, I started feeling better. I had days pain free and also set backs because as soon as I started feeling better, I felt too comfortable with my back and started doing activities that my back was not ready for. Dr. Donath assured me that if I slowed down I was going to feel better in a few days, and I did. I am now completely pain free!

I appreciate all the care and personal attention that the staff and the doctors have shown me during the difficult process of recovery. I highly recommend Dr. Donath and his practice.

Michael D. -White Plains, NY

Being a 25 year old mixed martial arts fighter I am always putting my body at risk for serious injuries. One day while sparring with a partner I took an unexpected fall on top of my head. I immediately felt pain and numbness racing down my shoulder and into my right arm and thumb. I continued to train in constant pain for 6 months. During that time I racked up more shoulder and neck injuries until I could barely turn my head. The constant pain and numbness were unbearable.

I searched the web for a solution in my area and discovered Dr. Donath. Dr. Donath seemed like a very knowledgeable doctor so I agreed to get the MRI and find out what was really wrong with me. The MRI showed that I had severely ruptured a cervical disc at C5-C6 and it was having a massive effect on a nerve. I also had trapped nerves in my chest and shoulder that were adding to the pain.

Dr. Donath treated me with spinal decompression as well as active release therapy. In the beginning I didn't notice much of a difference and then a few weeks into treatment I woke up without pain. I was easily able to turn my head again and the numbness was completely gone.

I really believe that if I had just had spinal decompression without active release therapy I wouldn't have had half the results. Dr. Donath's hands on techniques work. He knew exactly which techniques were going to work. He is an amazing doctor and can help with all of your neck and shoulder problems. I am certain if it weren't for him, I would have needed surgery.

Steven E. -White Plains, NY

I wanted to let you know how pleased I am that I came to your practice back in November of 2007. As you know, I had been suffering for a number of months from what I thought was a reoccurrence of some nerve pain that was from surgery I had back in 1975. The pain in my legs was waking me up at night, keeping me awake and my legs were very weak to the point that walking was slow and painful.

At the suggestion of my spouse, I came to you to seek out an alternative treatment that might be able to give me relief. After meeting with you and discussing the alternatives, I decided to move forward with the spinal decompression. Because of the pain I was in I put my faith in you that this could make a significant difference in not only how I felt, but with my overall body motion. After I had the MRI, you were able to focus on the source of the pain, which was actually a new ruptured disc...not from my older injury.

Even though it took a bit longer to get to the point that I knew I was getting some relief, I am glad I stuck it out! Today, I am 99% better, with almost all of the pain from my legs gone. I have a much better range of motion, am stronger and resumed skiing and playing golf. I can say that without this treatment I would have not been where I am today. I would certainly recommend this treatment and your services to anyone with similar problems.
Thank you for everything.

Abe A. -White Plains, NY

I had a herniated disc in my neck at section C-6-7 which was impinging on my nerve on the left side. I had numbness in my left arm/hand and severe pain in my neck and left shoulder. I had tried many other treatments. I had 3 deep injections by a pain specialist. I had seen two different spine surgeons who both recommended that I have surgery to remove the disc in my neck. I had also tried physical therapy and nothing worked. The pain I experienced was so severe that I couldn't work, and while waiting for my MRI results to make the decision on surgery, I heard about Non-Surgical Spinal Decompression. I had 22 sessions with Dr. Donath, in which I felt immediate relief after the first treatment. I'm able to work now, and the pain was reduced significantly. Treatment was painless, actually rather enjoyable. I would recommend it to others who have similar symptoms.

Jaami A. -Jamaica Hills, NY

I have been having lower back pain since I sprained it in my early thirties. From that time, I received physical and massage therapy for about a year. My pain did go away but my back stiffened and I became a wonderful patron of the ICY HOT products.

Eventually, my back improved, however fast forward a few years later, I discovered I had a herniated and degenerative disc disease. My pain was excruciating, I could not stand, bend, lift, without feeling jolts of pain. In association with this pain was severe numbness and tingling which radiated throughout my body up until I saw Dr. Donath.

At the onset of the pain, my neurologist recommended muscle relaxer pills, numerous physical therapy consultations. However, when none of it worked, I was referred to a neurosurgeon who recommended surgery. Therefore, I began to scour the internet to seek alternative treatments. I had heard about spinal decompression and I decided to research it on YouTube and that's when I discovered Dr. Donath's practice.

After my first consultation, I felt 50 percent better. Then after the 3rd, 100% better. It was a miracle, but in all honesty, the skeptic inside of me waited for the pain to return but it didn't. The treatments were so good that I traveled 3 ½ hours each way from Queens to White Plains just to get the Spinal Decompression treatment because I had to take public transportation. However, all my efforts were worth it because the pain dramatically reduced and I returned to physical activities that I enjoyed and fulfilled me without severe aches and pain.

Mike A. -Scarsdale, NY

I am 52-years old and have suffered upper-back and neck pain since I was in high school. I have tried chiropractors of various disciplines, and physical therapy, but these provided temporary relief at best. I was told I needed surgery for herniated discs several years ago, but I felt that since I had lived with the pain for so long already, the risks out-weighed any potential gains. Mostly, I had just learned to live with the pain. I went to see Dr. Donath when the pain began to increase in both intensity and frequency. I was losing my ability to concentrate at work and it was interfering with sleep. I noticed improvement in my range of motion after the first session and a renewed sense of energy at work. Improvement was pretty steady every week. After about 7 weeks, I no longer feel pain upon waking every morning. Seriously, I feel as if I'm at least 10-years younger.

Nina D. -White Plains, NY

I was walking my dog and she chased after a squirrel and yanked so hard on the leash that my neck jerked. It steadily grew more stiff and painful, so I went to urgent care. The nurse mis-diagnosed me with "muscle spasms" and gave me pills. They made me feel drugged and lethargic and the stiffness and pain still got worse. Fortunately, I made her refer me to a chiropractor, just to be sure, and she gave me Dr. Donath's number, (but only because a Doctor at Westchester Medical was seeing him and recommended him to her.)

Very quickly I could tell Dr. Donath knew his stuff. The pain by now was a 9/10 on the pain scale, but the first hands on treatment he gave me reduced it immediately and gave me some movement back. Within a few days, I had an MRI and was starting daily decompression therapy, (which I love) to treat the herniated disc. Recovery was extremely quick and enjoyable. They play your choice of music and let you relax. After the first week the pain went down to 6/10, by the second 4/10 and by the third 2/10. I was pain free and had full movement after a month. All the staff are so warm, relaxed and friendly, in person and on the phone, and everyone has a good sense of humor. I enjoy going there and feel nurtured and cared for in every way. I am so blessed to have been treated by such professional and kind people. Thank you Donath team.

Rabbi Reuven F. -New Rochelle, NY

After decades of chronic back and neck pain I had learned to live with the pain. After trying various interventions including chiropractic, traction, rehabilitation, meditation, and even acupuncture which did not work, I gave up. I heard about Dr. Donath from an acquaintance who is a physician. He suffered from severe back pain for years. He said that he was cured by Dr. Donath. I skeptically contacted Dr. Donath. Even though I was immediately impressed by his warm smile and obvious competence, I remained skeptical about his ability to help me. The doubts were erased after just a few sessions. The pain "miraculously" disappeared. With maintenance and the excellent exercise regimen I hope to remain pain free. Thank you Dr. Donath for all you did for me and for others. You are a truly compassionate healer.

Tanya T. -Brooklyn, NY

Before seeing Dr. Donath, I had been having terrible wrist pain for well over a year, strange burning sensations in various parts of my legs and eventually I developed a very stiff but not often painful neck. A neurologist scared me half to death when he suggested that I might have Multiple Sclerosis. During this evaluation, they discovered two herniated discs in my neck. I asked the neurologist if this could cause my wrist pain and burning sensations. He said, "No" rather emphatically. When I told Dr. Donath my story he seemed instantly to know that all of my complaints were being caused by the herniated discs in my neck and with great confidence told me that he could help me. He did ART (Active Release

Techniques) to get my wrist in better shape. I saw results immediately. I eventually did spinal decompression for my stiff neck and after one visit, I noticed a significant reduction in the stiffness and burning sensations and after only 3 or 4 treatments, I had total relief. Two years later, I have only mild and sporadic pain and an occasional visit keeps me feeling great.

Jonathan M. -Pelham, NY

I was suffering from increasing back pain that was more and more preventing me from standing straight. I contacted my orthopedist who probably saw me as a surgery candidate (which I wanted to avoid). Luckily, he was not immediately available. My internist recommended that I visit Dr. Donath. Dr. Donath returned my call the same day and invited me in for a consult the next day. After reviewing my MRI, Dr. Donath prescribed a regimen of spinal decompression, exercise, and nutritional supplements. I am a passionate recreational golfer and I have played competitively for three years. Dr. Donath predicted that I would be swinging a golf club in eight weeks and be on my way to a full recovery in twelve weeks. I nearly cried because the prospect seemed so dim. I am now at the twelve week mark and Dr. Donath's predictions for recovery were not overstated. I began with three to four treatments per week. After three weeks I was standing straight with relatively little pain and stiffness. At that time I began my exercises. After six weeks, I began playing golf again and moved to twice per week treatments. At ten weeks I moved to once per week and I am now moving to once every other week. While I still have some lingering pain, it continues to get less as time goes by. I practice my golf nearly every day and I have little discomfort. I am extremely pleased with the results of the treatment and I believe it would not have been possible without Dr. Donath and the prescribed regimen.

Maria S. -White Plains, NY

I was diagnosed with a herniated disc in my lower back. I tried different treatments, but no one was able to help me. I did a lot of research about which therapies I should use and there was one about the DTS machine that really got my attention. I had my first consultation with Dr. Donath in which he was so confident that I would get my life back together. Other doctors told me that I had a lifelong condition and I would be very limited in what I could do. From the beginning, I was very skeptical that the DTS machine would help me. After all, how could a machine help relieve the pain and the pressure that I had in my lower back for so long. Out of desperation, I decided to try it. For the first 2 weeks I didn't get much better, but after the 3rd week all the pressure was moving to different areas and by the end of the sessions I felt completely better. Now several months later, I feel like a new person, I've gone back to my normal life and doing things that I was not supposed to be able to do. From my own experience I strongly recommend people who have this condition try Spinal Decompression Therapy. The therapy does not hurt and I felt relaxed the whole time.

Robert T. -White Plains, NY

Dr. Donath is a true professional in every sense of the word. My first impression of Dr. Donath was of a doctor who was caring, sincere, and genuinely concerned about one's well-being. I have grown to appreciate and respect his professional advice and treatments. I am being treated for a herniated disc problem in both my neck as well as my back. Dr. Donath took the time to explain what caused my problems and the options available to resolve the pain I had been experiencing for so long. The pain I used to feel is almost completely gone and the numbness I used to feel into my hands is significantly better.

It is not every day that you meet a person/doctor who you feel comfortable with right from the beginning; Dr. Donath is a professional who I trust, respect and never doubt his integrity at any time. I feel fortunate to have met a doctor who has my best interest in mind and has become a friend who is always there if you need him. I have been blessed to have found Dr. Donath who tries to keep me healthy and pain-free.

Ann Marie H. -Peekskill, NY

I have had on and off back pain for many years. But this last time it did not get better and I also had spasmodic leg pain. After a MRI, I was diagnosed with a large herniated disc and spinal stenosis. I tried various treatments including acupuncture and epidurals which provided very temporary relief. The pain was constant and I was taking medication daily and was seriously considering surgery. While googling for more information on stenosis, I came across Dr. Donath's ad for spinal decompression therapy.

The decision to call and come in for a consultation turned out to be a great one. Although it took longer than initially thought for me to get completely better, Dr. Donath and his staff did not give up on me and today I am pain free.